How to Build the Church of the Future

How to Build the Church of the Future

20 Years of Inclusive Church

Edited by Ruth Wilde
Foreword by Rachel Mann

scm press

© Editor and contributors 2023

Published in 2023 by SCM Press
Editorial office
3rd Floor, Invicta House,
108–114 Golden Lane,
London EC1Y 0TG, UK

www.scmpress.co.uk

SCM Press is an imprint of Hymns Ancient & Modern Ltd
(a registered charity)

Hymns Ancient & Modern® is a registered trademark of
Hymns Ancient & Modern Ltd
13A Hellesdon Park Road, Norwich,
Norfolk NR6 5DR, UK

All rights reserved. No part of this publication may be reproduced,
stored in a retrieval system, or transmitted,
in any form or by any means, electronic, mechanical,
photocopying or otherwise, without the prior permission of
the publisher, SCM Press.

The editor and contributors have asserted their right under the
Copyright, Designs and Patents Act 1988 to be identified as the
Authors of this Work

The Scripture quotations contained herein are from The New Revised
Standard Version of the Bible, Anglicized Edition, copyright © 1989,
1995 by the Division of Christian Education of the National Council
of the Churches of Christ in the United States of America, and are
used by permission. All rights reserved.

British Library Cataloguing in Publication data

A catalogue record for this book is available
from the British Library

ISBN 978-0-334-06519-7

Typeset by Regent Typesetting
Printed and bound by
CPI Group (UK) Ltd

Contents

Contributors   vii
Foreword by Rachel Mann   ix
Introduction by Dan Barnes-Davies   xi

1. What is Inclusion? *by Ruth Wilde*   1
2. Belonging Together *by Michael Jagessar*   11
3. Building Bridges *by Ruth Hunt*   23
4. Poverty Has a Woman's Face *by Loretta Minghella*   32
5. Dismantling Whiteness and Deconstructing Mission Christianity *by Anthony Reddie*   47
6. Still Calling from the Edge *by Fiona MacMillan*   58
7. What Might a Trans-Affirming Church Look Like? *by Jack Woodruff*   72
8. Carnival and Chaos! *by June Boyce-Tillman*   81
9. The Church of the Future *by Ruth Wilde*   97

Epilogue – Beyond Inclusion – An Interview with Nick Bundock   108

Index   119

Contributors

Dan Barnes-Davies is the Chair of Inclusive Church and a Vicar for Barry in the Church in Wales.

June Boyce-Tillman is a priest, university professor, theologian, musician, author and prolific hymn writer.

Nick Bundock is Rector of St James and Emmanuel in Didsbury, Manchester and founder of Didsbury Pride.

Ruth Hunt was CEO of Stonewall until 2019. Since then, she has set up and been running her own consultancy firm, Deeds and Words, with her partner Caroline Ellis.

Michael Jagessar is a minister in the United Reformed Church, who was for many years responsible for intercultural ministries in that denomination. He is now a freelance writer and researcher.

Fiona MacMillan is Chair of the Disability Accessibility Group at St Martin-in-the-Fields and Vice-Chair of Inclusive Church. She is also Chair of the planning team for the annual Conference on Disability and Church (a partnership between Inclusive Church and St Martin-in-the-Fields).

Loretta Minghella was CEO of Christian Aid from 2010 to 2017. She is now Master of Clare College, Cambridge.

Anthony Reddie is Director of the Centre for Religion and Culture at Regent's Park College, Oxford. He is also an Extraordinary Professor of Theological Ethics at the University of South Africa. He is the UK's leading Black Liberation theologian.

Ruth Wilde is National Coordinator of Inclusive Church and Tutor for the Inclusion of Disabled People at Northern Baptist College.

Jack Woodruff is an Inclusive Church trustee and a contributor to the book *Young, Woke and Christian* (2022).

Foreword

RACHEL MANN

'God is really weird.' It's probably not the tag-line or mission statement that Inclusive Church – as it celebrates twenty fantastic years – is likely to adopt for its next decade or two. Nonetheless, as I read this book and was impressed by its many striking turns of phrase and theological gambits, it was that phrase (used by IC National Coordinator Ruth Wilde) which would not let me go. It captures something of the extraordinary otherness of God and gestures towards his/her/their passionate longing for the flourishing of Creation and the Church. 'God is really weird.' It reminds me that any kind of work the People of God undertake to make the Church more inclusive, hopeful and celebratory of difference has to treat with a God who exceeds our attempts at domestication. The God who loves and delights in us is not cosy; she blows our minds and invites us to feast around the most expansive table.

Part of what makes Inclusive Church's mission and work so important is how it effects change at the congregational and local level. As this local work happens, I believe it acts like yeast in the bread of the wider Church, expanding and enriching the Church's possibilities. That which was flat becomes three-dimensional; that which was bland becomes food which satisfies. I've witnessed how transformative this work can be: I've seen LGBTQ+ people's bodies relax when they realize they've found a church in which their lives are cherished. I've seen how disabled and neurodivergent people, and so many others, can challenge the status quo and hold a church to account because it has signed up to Inclusive Church. When I was in parish ministry, I found leading an inclusive church and being Area Dean of an inclusive deanery was not always easy and never bland. There was disagreement and friction. This was no holy huddle of the like-minded. The friction, however, kept us warm and I took it as a sign of hope.

The work of inclusion, then, is not passive, but active; it is not about niceness, but God's radical grace and love. Inclusion work desires a new world and seeks to make a new world, more faithful to God – the God who is ever ancient and ever new – than we can imagine. In the midst of the hard-won, practical work undertaken by all of us committed to Inclusive Church is an invitation into the divine mystery of God. This mystery is captured for me in our call, both as communities and individuals, to participate in and be transformed by Jesus Christ. My sense is that as we travel further with and deeper into the mystery of the God who is the ultimate other, and whose love exceeds all human calculation, we encounter the One who cherishes our particular differences and yet calls us into something which shatters dogma, dominion and division.

I wholeheartedly commend this book. It is itself an invitation to challenge and hope; it will offer both comfort and disruption; it will set your heart on fire for justice and help each of us to feel better equipped to address the emerging questions and opportunities as we travel on into Inclusive Church's next decade of work. The work of justice, hope and grace is never done, not in this age anyway. However, as this book shows, so much has already been accomplished. As we acknowledge and celebrate those achievements, we look to one another in solidarity and to the Living God in hope as we ready ourselves for the challenges still to come.

Canon Rachel Mann
Christmas 2022

Introduction

DAN BARNES-DAVIES

I'm not totally sure where it all began. It might have been on 28 January 2012. I have an event in my electronic calendar that day called 'YIC', at Short Street, London. For a little while, there was a group called Young Inclusive Church, which met at St Andrew's Church, Waterloo. I don't even remember how I found out about this meeting, but I suspect I was looking to fill a hole in my life which resembled my university chaplaincy. That is to say: a community of Christians where I wouldn't have to be constantly vigilant for undercurrents of homophobia and other exclusions. I think that the group's convenor at the time attended Inclusive Church's trustee board on our behalf, but at some point he wasn't able to continue, so I took over that role from him. Alas, YIC tailed off as things sometimes do, but by then I was already 'hooked'.

I stood for election as an independent trustee (as we call those trustees not representing partner organizations). I received a warm welcome from my fellow trustees, and they were kind and patient with their (very young) new comrade. Through things like board meetings, our Greenbelt stand, partnership days and Annual Lectures, the community of Inclusive Church drew me in. I am a white, straight, cis man of British heritage, not to mention middle-class; and at that time, I didn't identify as disabled. I didn't bring lived experience of marginalization. I was keen – and odd – and I was still learning to listen to people who had that lived experience. Over ten years later, I am the longest-serving current trustee and Chair of the board.

Why? Why should it be that *this* organization has kept my attention for so long, through a period of great change in my own life? I have been through the Church of England's selection process, trained, been ordained deacon and priest, served as curate, married, moved to Wales and become a father. I think it's the knowledge that I am a small part of a large and ever-growing movement; that in all corners of England, and throughout these isles, and, yes, even the whole world, we are a network dedicated to the Christlike service of the 'other'. Most individual members, or members of our churches, will have lived experience of discrimination on one basis or another (or experience of intersectional discrimination) – even if perhaps some don't recognize it yet.

For as long as I can remember, I've described Inclusive Church as an 'umbrella organization' – we bring together groups and individuals with different experiences of exclusion and, together, try to work for the inclusion of all. I think I first started to understand this when I helped out with one of our earliest annual disability conferences at St Martin-in-the-Fields. That year, and every conference since, I have learned a huge amount about what it means to live as a disabled person. When, a few years later, my own neurodivergence was diagnosed, that community was radically welcoming and genuinely encouraging as I started to accept and embrace a part of my identity I hadn't previously been able to name. As it turned out, I *did* have experience of discrimination. I am white, so I cannot truly imagine what it's like to face racism every single day of my life; I am a man, so it is difficult for me to really grasp the visceral depths of misogyny which women face; and so forth. But as I came to recognize my own experiences of exclusion for what they were, and continued to face ongoing exclusion, I came to realize that this is what binds us together. Those of us who have any recognition of the systems of oppression we all face are – or ought to be – allies and comrades to each other. As some of the longer-running trustees have started to habitually say: 'All exclusion is the same exclusion'.

I can't count the number of times I've been told that Inclusive

INTRODUCTION

Church started as a single-issue campaign against homophobia in the Church of England; and that we only later broadened our horizons to oppose other forms of exclusion. Only in researching our origins for this very introduction did I realize how completely wrong that assertion is. It is true that the catalyst for what is now Inclusive Church was the resignation of Jeffrey John, whose appointment as area Bishop of Reading (in the Diocese of Oxford) had been announced on 20 May 2003.[1] Dr John had been with his (male) partner for about 30 years. Despite their public assurances of abstinence (as this was what the Church required of them), conservatives in England and throughout the worldwide Anglican Communion cried havoc. On 6 July, the Diocese of Oxford published a short letter from Dr John announcing his intention not to take up the See.[2] On 10 August, the church news site Thinking Anglicans (itself only one day old) carried the press release 'Grassroots Church movement calls for Inclusiveness',[3] which announced the next day's meeting and Eucharist. 'The meeting is an occasion for Christians to express their views over issues such as the Jeffrey John debacle and the Church's resistance to women bishops', it stated.

The late Colin Slee, then Dean of Southwark, preached that day at St Mary's Putney,[4] and a petition was launched for an inclusive Church. Even before that first public meeting, the inclusion of women in the Church's ministry was at the forefront of the organizers' minds alongside LGBTQI+ inclusion. On 15 September, the organization Inclusive Church was formed, with an interim steering group including Giles Fraser (then Vicar of Putney) as Chair;[5] and on 6 October, the Executive Committee formally constituted the organization (then regularly referred to by its URL and in the then-prevalent CamelCase style as 'InclusiveChurch'). The committee resolved to register with the Charity Commission.[6] On 10 February 2004, the petition was handed to Chris Smith, chief of staff to Rowan Williams (then Archbishop of Canterbury) in Dean's Yard, outside Church House Westminster, where the General Synod of the Church of England meets.[7] It numbered 'over 8000 individual supporters, over 100 PCCs and over 100 other organizations'.[8] In 2007, Clare Herbert was appointed our first National Coordinator (also called Programme Director). She served until 2010, when she was succeeded by Bob Callaghan. After Bob's departure in 2017, Ruth Wilde became the third and current National Coordinator in 2018. The three Chairs previous to me were Giles Fraser (until 2005), Giles Goddard (2005–12) and Dianna Gwilliams (2012–22).

In the earliest days, the overwhelming focus was on issues such as women bishops and gay bishops in the Anglican Communion, but I think that the real turning point at which the central organization of Inclusive Church started to broaden our focus was the first joint Disability Conference with St Martin-in-the-Fields. Though she would be the first to highlight the hard work of dozens of members over the past decade, the truth is that these conferences could not have happened without the commitment and dedicated work of Fiona MacMillan (chair of SMITF Disability Advisory Group, Chair of the Disability Conference planning group and IC trustee). Through our involvement in this and other projects, such as Mental Health Matters with the Church of England (especially through Eva Mcintyre), our partnerships – and therefore our understanding of inclusion – were opened out.

In the last few years, we have also been making conscious efforts to become less Anglican-focused. It wasn't very long before non-Anglican/Episcopalian churches applied to register in our directory, and the decision was quickly made to include these churches in our network. In terms of partners, the 2003 press release named the groups sending representatives as 'LGCM [now OneBodyOneFaith], Changing Attitude, Affirming Catholicism, MCU [now Modern Church], GRAS [Group for Rescinding the Act of Synod] and the Open Synod group'.[9] Today, the groups which send partner trustees to the board of Inclusive Church include Women and the Church (WATCH), Open Table, the Student Christian Movement, HeartEdge and Modern Church. To look only at the list of formal partner organizations would be to ignore a vital source of our lifeblood,

INTRODUCTION

though – the diversity of the lived experiences brought by our various trustees, staff, regional ambassadors and supporters over the course of twenty years.

I've noted with historical interest that this organization was originally styled 'inclusivechurch.net' and 'InclusiveChurch'; but there is another version of our name which I believe deserves deeper inspection. Our current constitution is in fact headed 'Charity name: The Inclusive Church Network'. The October 2003 newsletter announcing the charity's formation also uses this word 'network': 'Essentially, Inclusive Church is a network of groups and individuals who are campaigning for an Inclusive Church.'[10] I have said on occasion that we have forgotten one-third of our own name! Perhaps it goes without saying that we are a network. I wonder – to how many people (inside and outside of our network) is IC just a thing to which a person, or church, signs up. As a long-time trustee, I can easily slip into thinking of IC as the strategic and governance role which the board undertakes (ably assisted by our talented staff), or the many staff activities which are reported back to us. All of that is, in truth, such a small fraction of what Inclusive Church *is* (and does), because neither the board nor the staff *are* IC. Perhaps the most important word in our name is the one which we seldom use, but which is nonetheless lived out every day across these isles and the world.

So we come to 2023, to our 20th anniversary year, and to this very book. In many ways, it's sad that Inclusive Church has reached 20. We have always been and always will be one of those charities which exists to make itself redundant. Yes, the Church of England now ordains women as bishops. But, as I write this, it has recently been announced that a bishop who doesn't ordain women is to become a diocesan bishop – for the first time since women started serving as bishops. Whatever any of us may think about the subtleties of the settlement, it is a matter of fact that women *still* don't serve in ministry in the Church of England on the same basis as their male colleagues (and that's without even mentioning people of minority gender identities). Between my writing and publication, General Synod is due to engage in the 'decision-making' phase of 'Living in Love and Faith' – the Church of England's latest effort to address (or delay addressing) matters of sexuality. Twenty years after the Reading affair, there is only one out gay bishop in the Church of England – and he was outed almost a year *after* his appointment, at which point he (and people on his behalf) gave strenuous assurances of abstinence.

There are many ways in which the Church which birthed Inclusive Church has barely changed. But Inclusive Church has changed, in the ways I've examined and in many others. We now embrace supporters and registered churches from other denominations (and none) which are more institutionally free to celebrate the fabulous diversity of God's wonderful creation. Even as certain churches have barely made progress (at least in some areas), the world we inhabit has continued to learn and to teach more. Our understanding of the glorious breadth of the LGBTQ+ spectrum is growing every day; the Black Lives Matter movement has been a watershed moment in the public discourse around race; and understanding of mental health and disabilities – including neurodiversity – is increasing. At the same time, resistance to equity and inclusion persists. I'm sure dozens of books are being written on this, and I am no sociologist. I am a priest. Perhaps I am even a prophet on a good day. As such, what I can say is that the Holy Spirit blows where she will; and she wills justice. She wants equity for all people.

If I am a prophet, it's because I am a small part of this movement; because I am one node in a network which has been calling to the Church for 20 years. Our prophecy is that the image of God dwells deeply in every single person, so God calls the Church to inclusion. God calls the Church to so value God's image in every person that we cannot help but love them, and miss them when they are not there. The chapters which follow examine in much greater depth some of the ways in which the Church can and should seek greater inclusion, equity and justice. Thank you for choosing to read, and thank you for being part of this movement.

Fr Dan Barnes-Davies, SCP, Chair of Inclusive Church

INTRODUCTION

Notes

1 https://web.archive.org/web/20030802105959/http://www.oxford.anglican.org/detail.php?id=421 (accessed 17.4.23).
2 https://web.archive.org/web/20030724200644/http://www.oxford.anglican.org/detail.php?id=475 (accessed 17.4.23).
3 https://www.thinkinganglicans.org.uk/67-2/ (accessed 17.4.23).
4 https://www.thinkinganglicans.org.uk/74-2/ (accessed 4.5.23).
5 http://web.archive.org/web/20031016010814/http://www.inclusivechurch.net/aboutus.shtml (accessed 4.5.23).
6 http://web.archive.org/web/20031016011437/http://www.inclusivechurch.net/newsletter.shtml (accessed 4.5.23).
7 *Church Times*, 13 February 2004 page 3 (picture caption).
8 http://web.archive.org/web/20040401223751/http://www.inclusivechurch.net:80/index.shtml (accessed 4.5.23).
9 Ibid.; https://www.thinkinganglicans.org.uk/67-2/.
10 Ibid.; http://web.archive.org/web/20031016011437/http://www.inclusivechurch.net/newsletter.shtml.

1

What is Inclusion?

RUTH WILDE[1]

Inclusion is ... Being Valued, Loved, Respected

In 2015, Inclusive Church had a stall at Greenbelt, as it often does. It was before my time, when Bob Callaghan was the National Coordinator, but I remember it well. I was there with my wife, Ellie, and we'd recently celebrated our first wedding anniversary. We've been every year since the year we met at one of the LGBTQ+ 'Outerspace' events. Of course, when I say 'every year', I mean every year apart from 2020 and 2021, when it didn't happen due to the Covid-19 pandemic. That was a terrible time for so many reasons.

On the stall that year, Bob had placed postcards with the words 'inclusion is ...' on them, followed by a blank space for people to write their thoughts. I found out later that Bob saved every single postcard and took an individual picture of each one. They are still in the folders that were passed on to me. To give a flavour, here are some of the things people wrote:

- Inclusion is ... feeling valued, loved and respected for who you are.
- Inclusion is ... all people on an equal footing.
- Inclusion is ... the freedom to be yourself, who God made you to be.
- Inclusion is ... taking time and thought to understand where others are coming from.
- Inclusion is ... friendship.

These thoughts from different festival-goers are so simple and yet so profound. Sometimes we don't need to say things in a complicated way, because the truth is simply that God calls, loves and values every one of us. Every single one. When the Church tells people otherwise or says that certain people need to change who they are intrinsically to be allowed in, that message is not of God and it is not of the Kingdom. If anyone is excluded, the Church is not being what the Church is meant to be. God will simply build the Church somewhere else, without us.

Inclusion is essential because of all the reasons given above and more. We get an equally, if not more, powerful message if we put what the postcards say the other way round. They read as a prophetic wake-up call for a Church which has for so long excluded and marginalized many people:

- Exclusion is when we do not value those God values, do not love those God loves, and do not respect those God respects (which is to say, everyone).
- Exclusion is when we do not allow people to be on an equal footing with others. It is when we tell some people that they are 'less than' others and encourage them to internalize hatred of themselves for the way they are – whether that's for the colour of their skin, their sexuality, their disability or anything else about them they can't change.
- Exclusion is preventing people from being themselves, from being who God made them to be. It is robbing people of their God-given identity, their self-worth and their integrity. It is forcing them to conform via coercion and threat. It is a 'system headed by a dictator in which the [governing body] controls ... and opposition is not permitted'. Some people have called this 'Christofascism'. If you think that is a bit extreme, just know that the quote I used just now is from the Merriam-Webster dictionary definition of fascism.
- Exclusion is ignoring people's stories and dismissing their experiences. It is telling them that they don't matter and what they feel isn't real. Some might call this 'gaslighting'. It is tell-

ing people what we think about them rather than listening to what they want to tell us about themselves.
- Exclusion is being the enemies of our siblings in Christ.

Inclusive Church's call since its formation in 2003 has been to resist the powers of division, enmity and exclusion, and to instead value, love, respect and empower those who have been marginalized. We believe inclusion is a core component of the gospel. That is why our vision statement goes like this:

> We believe in inclusive church – a church which celebrates and affirms every person and does not discriminate. We will continue to challenge the church where it continues to discriminate against people on grounds of disability, economic power, ethnicity, gender, gender identity, learning disability, mental health, neurodiversity, or sexuality. We believe in a church which welcomes and serves all people in the name of Jesus Christ; which is scripturally faithful; which seeks to proclaim the Gospel afresh for each generation; and which, in the power of the Holy Spirit, allows all people to grasp how wide and long and high and deep is the love of Jesus Christ. (IC Vision Statement updated in 2019)

Inclusion is ... Embracing Otherness

My sister sent me an image online a while ago of different angels described in the Bible and how strange they are. It made me laugh out loud. I would recommend that anyone who is curious just Googles 'seraphim' to see what comes up! Some of the angels in the Bible are extremely bizarre and a little bit frightening when drawn exactly as described. In Isaiah 6.1–8, the angels are described as having six wings – two covering their eyes, two covering their feet and two for flying. These angels also have hands, it seems, as they put the coal on Isaiah's lips with a hand.

This is not the place to consider the literalism of this Bible story, and no doubt there is symbolism in the covering of the eyes and feet which is far more important than any literal understanding of the passage. However, the point I want to make is this one: God's angels are really weird! And that's because *God* is really weird. God is completely unfathomable to us and different to anything we can really grasp. Although there are many passages in the Bible where God is a comfort to people, there are also many passages where angels have to tell people to not be afraid, and where God appears in burning bushes and the like (see Luke 1.13, Luke 1.30, Matthew 28.5 and Exodus 3). Part of the awe-inspiring, fear-inspiring nature of God lies in God's extreme otherness – extreme weirdness.

In a recent survey, a majority of people said they were too afraid to speak to disabled people because they didn't know what to say to them.[2] This fear leads to disabled people being isolated in church and society. Far too often, wheelchair users are spoken over and ignored.

LGBTQ+ people are another group that seem to terrify the Church. The presence of queer people can produce the most extreme reactions. Sensible churchgoers and otherwise loving parents can be reduced to name-calling bullies in the presence of LGBTQ+ people.

There are many other marginalized groups that people fear. This fear is, at heart, a fear of the other. However, if we are able to worship a God who is wholly and completely other, we really should be able to cope with and get used to fellow human beings who look, marry or get around differently to us. Fear is a natural reaction to change and difference, but we need to move through it. Inclusion necessitates discomfort. If we're not uncomfortable at having to change as a Church, we're not doing inclusion right. So many churches long for young people or more diverse congregations, but when different people appear, with all their different needs, wishes and ways of doing things, the congregation goes into meltdown and shuts them out or places them in a safe box where they can't change the Church in any real way or have any real influence on the 'way things have always been'.

WHAT IS INCLUSION?

Inclusion is about calling. If we are not being inclusive, we are not being the Church, because God calls everyone, and if we put barriers up and reject people whom God is calling, we are not building the Kingdom of God; we are not doing what God is doing; we are not being the Church. Who are we to say who is or is not called by God? Anyone and everyone can be called by God – not just to take part or get in the Church, but to lead in the Church too. We must break down barriers, not put them up.

Inclusion means firstly overcoming our fear of difference in order to learn and grow. Secondly, it means realizing that we can't be the Church if we are not inclusive, because God calls everyone. Finally, inclusion means looking to the future, because the future of the Church is inclusive. It *has* to be, or it is not doing God's work. Inclusion is a gospel imperative. Jesus mixed with everyone, included everyone and called everyone. His ragtag group of fishermen and tax collectors were called, despite the judgemental looks from a society which preferred exclusion and comfortable boxes for people to stay in and be controlled in. The future of the Church must also be inclusive, because if it is not it will die. Young people do not want to have anything to do with a Church which does not involve and include all people. Recent research from the Methodist Church showed that one of the main things growing churches had in common is that they were inclusive.[3] There were other factors, but they all had inclusion in common. It is not just the right thing to do; it is the pragmatic thing to do too.

Inclusion might feel uncomfortable and hard at first, but it is a huge blessing in the long run. All the churches I speak to who have been on a journey towards being more inclusive say this. Some churches have been through difficult times, even painful ones, but they all come out the other end being blessed by angels in their midst they didn't even know were there. The Church has long excluded and rejected people it thought were broken and wrong in some way, but it is the Church which is broken and incomplete without all of its members (as Paul would have it). Paul himself most likely had a disability – something he terms the 'thorn in his side'[4] – so he will have known what it was like to be different and to be considered less than others. It is the Church which is less, which is not whole, which is not really the Church when it excludes certain people from the call of God.

Inclusion is ... Learning From Marginalized Peoples

I always love a challenge when preaching. When I am given a difficult reading, it gives me an opportunity to wrestle with scripture, which we are all called to do. Jesus himself loved to wrestle with and argue with scripture. He interpreted the scriptures in new ways, and asked questions of the society he was in (e.g. Matthew 5.38–48). Once, when preparing to preach in a church in Halesowen, I was given the lectionary readings and one of them was the story of blind Bartimaeus (Mark 10.46–52). As the representative of a charity which puts on a pioneering Conference on Disability and Church with our partner, St Martin-in-the-Fields, each year, I felt this reading was a good one to tackle head-on.

The healing stories in the Bible have long been used as an excuse to treat disabled people as objects of pity and as broken people in need of healing, with no gifts or agency of their own. The Church has a long legacy of seeing disabled people at best as receptacles of charity, and at worst as products of sin. A priest I know told me that he still has the experience of people asking him randomly in the street why God hasn't healed him – especially when he's wearing his dog collar. Another person I know who is autistic has been told in a church that she needs to be broken down and built up again from scratch. A third friend told me she is never considered for leadership positions in church and is spoken down to like a child, because she uses a wheelchair. It can be thoroughly soul-destroying to be a disabled person in the Church.

When we hear a reading like this one about blind Bartimaeus, it's easy to feel angry about it and wish that it just didn't exist

WHAT IS INCLUSION?

in the lectionary, or perhaps even in the Bible. We can't impose our own culture and modern understanding of the world on first-century customs and beliefs, but we *can* wrestle with the scriptures and we *can* repent of the ways scripture has been used to hurt, harm and marginalize people.

In fact, the tragic irony of marginalizing disabled people by using passages like this one is that Jesus was very much performing a miracle here in order to *put a stop to* the marginalization of a man who was rejected by his community and begging on the side of the road. We don't have to assume that the best way to deal with disability nowadays is to go around attempting to heal people. Or at least not from their conditions anyway! Healing is something we all need, whether disabled or not.

Once we understand that the Bible is far from perfect in terms of the attitudes to disability within it, and the time of Jesus was very different to now, there are some really important things we can take from this reading. First, the blind man is named. Bartimaeus, son of Timaeus. Naming is quite significant in the Bible – his name has been remembered for some reason here. Perhaps he became important as part of the early Christian community later on, so his name was retained. That would also make sense of the fact that he follows Jesus at the end of the story. Jesus soon after this enters Jerusalem and is welcomed with palm leaves on the ground – this is the beginning of the end of the road for Jesus. Did Bartimaeus stay with Jesus until the end? It is interesting to note that, although in many parts of the New Testament blindness is equated with sin and a refusal to see things as they really are, in 2 Corinthians 5.7, Paul equates blindness with faith: 'For we walk by faith, not by sight', he says. Bartimaeus had a great faith, as Jesus says later in the story. Perhaps his faith continued to grow later on in his life too, as he continued to follow Jesus.

Naming is important for another reason too, when thinking about disability. Disabled people are people. People with names and lives. I know this sounds obvious, but it is not that obvious when you look at how they are sometimes treated in society. I have heard of wheelchair-using friends being forgotten on trains by guards, being shouted at for taking up space on the bus, and being constantly spoken over and ignored because people prefer to speak to the person pushing them when they're in a manual wheelchair. The way our society views disabled people differently when it comes to abortion and euthanasia is shocking. Babies are allowed to be aborted until they are coming down the birth canal in the UK, but only if they have Down's syndrome, and there are many popular films, like *Me Before You*, where disability is painted as something so tragic that you might as well kill yourself if you acquire a life-altering condition. Society in these instances says to disabled people: you do not matter, you are not even a person really, you do not deserve to be alive. So, yes, naming Bartimaeus is important.

The second thing I think we can take from this reading is that Bartimaeus was not shy in advocating for himself, despite the crowd attempting to shout him down and shut him up. This still happens to disabled people today. It is extremely exhausting to constantly fight the system and the way things are in order to get things changed and made more accessible so that you can just live your life. Disabled people are made to feel like nuisances every day simply for wanting to access services like public transport or to enter buildings. Good on Bartimaeus for not giving up and not giving in, but it's not always easy. It shouldn't only be up to disabled people themselves to advocate. Others of us should pay attention to what is needed to make the world a better place, and we should persistently ask and advocate alongside disabled people. Let's *all* be nuisances, so disabled people don't have to be made to feel that way.

The third and final point I want to take from this reading as I wrestle with it, is that Jesus' question to Bartimaeus is *liberating* for a disabled person. He asks, 'What do you want me to do?' Asking this question of disabled people, instead of assuming we know best and patronizing them, is empowering. It is what every disabled person hopes for from other people they meet. Disabled people themselves are the ones who know best what they need; not the government, and not the disabled person's friends or family. This question from Jesus shows Bartimaeus respect. It gives him agency and autonomy. It tells him 'I know you know best what you need'. It also – radically – does not just assume that the most important and only important thing to do is to heal Bartimaeus of his blindness. Jesus only gives him sight because that is what he asks for; not because Jesus thinks that's the one and only thing he needs.

Often the healing stories in the Gospels are more about healing from the wounds of rejection and marginalization – and bringing people who are excluded back into the community – than they are about making people physically 'normal'. It is impossible to read stories from the time of Jesus and to separate disability from social exclusion. Disabled people were socially excluded in Jesus' day. Jesus was often more concerned with healing relationships and bringing people back into the community group than with making disabled people non-disabled. Whether people were excluded because of disability or because of some other cultural 'transgression', Jesus wanted the community to accept them again, and there are many stories of him finding ways to make that happen. The Samaritan woman at the well, for example, in John 4, was accepted back into her community following Jesus' intervention.

If we want to be more inclusive, we should ask the same question of marginalized people that Jesus asked: 'What do you want me to do?' Another good question to ask is 'What is it you need from me/us as a church?' Or 'How can we make this church more accessible to you?' Also, 'How can we make you feel comfortable and included?' or 'What can we do better?' And so on. There are so many questions we can ask excluded and marginalized people – not only disabled people, but LGBTQ+ people, women, people of colour etc. The best way to find out how we can be more inclusive is by asking good questions. Educating ourselves is about being curious, especially about people who are different from us. If we take an interest in other people's experience and show a willingness to change and adapt so that marginalized people can be better included, rather than expecting everyone to adapt to us, we will grow and be enriched as a Church.

Notes

1 Parts of this chapter are adapted from sermons and talks Ruth has given at churches around the country.
2 www.scope.org.uk/media/press-releases/brits-feel-uncomfortable-with-disabled-people (accessed 15.5.23).
3 https://www.inclusive-church.org/wp-content/uploads/2020/05/22672.pdf.
4 See C. R. Moss (2012), 'Christly Possession and Weakened Bodies: Reconsideration of the Function of Paul's Thorn in the Flesh', *Journal of Religion, Disability and Health*, 16(4), pp. 319–33.

2

Belonging Together

MICHAEL JAGESSAR[1]

Locating Self and Crossing Over

I recently came across an underground advertisement which reads: 'On first impression, I may seem conservative.' It would be possible to substitute 'conservative' with 'progressive', 'radical' or any other descriptor. In spite of Malcolm Gladwell's book *Blink* (2005), first impressions can be deceptive in the world of complex identities. So let me partially undress myself in your company – as it may help locate my thoughts. I am a complex Caribbean Diasporan traveller – accidentally landing on these shores and largely welcomed by some friendly natives. While I am a minority in a majority context of the UK, I am also privileged (heterosexual, male, married, academic) within my minority context. My faith/spirituality has been informed and shaped by impulses from multiple religious and cultural traditions living in the fullness of two or three simultaneously. My God-talk (theology) is done within the rich world of diversity, identities, hybridity, impurity, many-one-ness, contradictions, fluidity, and 'tidalectics' (ebb and flow) Anansi-ism (Caribbean saint and trickster figure) – with all the exciting possibilities and challenges these offer.

I found a home in the dissenting, non-conforming and minority heritage of the United Reformed Church. As a minority church in three nations, the URC wrestles with identity issues, diversity and inclusion in all sorts of ways. While we may have lost our non-conforming vigour (genuflecting to the Status

Quo), we have not given up on good intentions of creating spaces to give agency to all sorts of minorities. I was elected as a moderator of our General Assembly (2012–14); however, this did not mean that belonging was reconfigured to include the difference and culturally shaped giftings I brought to the table. Everyone had to largely fit into a white, male, extroverted, heterosexual, non-disabled, English cultural framework. To find a place in church as a minority is somehow to be generally complicit with the dominant ethos. The habit of everyone around the table being mutually inconvenienced for the sake of economy of the host (God in Christ) remains uncomfortable and too demanding.

How do we move beyond representative minority voices and presence – break out of minority-ness to 'fuller participation' in our life together? *The Hundred-Foot Journey* (Helen Mirren, Om Puri, 2014) is an apt film on the challenges of belonging. It is the story of a migrant Mumbai family, whose whole life has been delighting in food and running a restaurant. Forced to move to the UK where they found the raw ingredients for food 'lacked soul', they decided to try Europe. When their old van breaks down in a sleepy South of France village, the father sees this as a sign that the family should stick around there and open an Indian restaurant (Maison Mumbai). Never mind the celebrated restaurant right across the street from their new premises, or the fact that they are in an insular part of the country. Papa Khaddam has faith in his food and in his son, Hassan – a brilliant young cook without a certificate. Hassan soon masters French cuisine and falls in love with the beautiful French chef Marguerite. The movie captures the tensions and interaction between cultures, generations, belonging and integration. Hassan doesn't just want to cook murgh masala with cashews and cardamom: he wants to belong to, and conquer, a new world. What comes through is the longing of the new voice around the table, the overwhelming push-pull between the need to belong, the constant reminder that you do not belong, and the need to assert one's own identity. The film is set in France where a genteel pride in the refinement and supremacy of one's own culture can easily be nudged into overt exclusion. Food serves to transcend bigotry, snobbery, prejudices, cultural and religious differences, and restrictive habits of every kind. Hassan learns to master béchamel and velouté sauce. Madame Mallory is eventually drawn across the road by the enchanting aroma of spices, even adding a dash of cardamom to her classic boeuf bourguignon. The two restaurants were 100 feet apart, but making the trip took a lot of effort at examining inherited traditions and rediscovering the joys of intercultural engagement in belonging together.

Table Space: Power and Privilege

A meal is a miniature of the 'whole gospel story' (Williams 2014). It is an ideal space to locate our thoughts beyond inclusion and on 'belonging together'. A meal is at the heart of our vocation to embrace the way of abundant life for all. Amy-Jill Levine writing in *The Misunderstood Jew* notes: 'The Kingdom of God is not a press conference, or a resolution, or a short course in how to be eloquently indignant. It is a table laden with grace, at which the social maps are all redrawn.'

Power is not necessarily evil; nor is it neutral. It is misused, though, when minority groups are disempowered and when dominant groups are empowered and privileged. We cannot help being privileged in contexts that are structured to give unfair advantages to the few. Who has power and who has privilege are two different questions. Power is held collectively within systems and structures. Privileges are afforded individuals who are part of the power structure. We must ask: for which group of people are the decision-making processes, along with the hierarchical structures, cultural values, educational materials, worship, hymns, liturgies and accountability arrangements in our Church historically created to favour? The answer is most likely a dominant group. Dominant groups operate in default ways – unconsciously inhabiting the privileges, internalizing it all. Marginalized groups can also internalize such a habit and then re-inscribe it. And, the identity of the dominant/normative group as superior is internalized as much as the inferiority of the marginalized group.

My experience as a theological educator in Britain, and as responsible both for intercultural ministries and moderating Councils of the United Reformed Church, is that power and privilege are often no-go areas, and convenient ways are found to allow these to remain intact through entitlement to rights and resources, knowledge production, comfort and attention, access to space, and deference. Even minorities are sucked into this pattern – and all while we give lip service to inclusion. In enabling diversity awareness processes, I have often found that participants are keener to name inequalities than to spend time interrogating the privilege machinery that produces the inequalities or to take steps countering them – especially if their own complicity and privilege are exposed. There is also an assumption that we operate on a level playing field where anyone can access the resources, means and space. This is a myth. In the teaching domain, colleagues representing the dominant group assume the right to dominate the space of theology and discussion. They assume the right to have attention and they assume this is nonreciprocal: others should be reading their work even while they neglect to read what we have written. I know you are gracious enough to excuse my generalizing and focus on the patterns I am trying to find words to describe, and that which we need to be aware of and challenge.

To understand what any form of marginalization does to minorities we need to explore and expose what it does to help dominant group(s). What can we do together to displace privilege and power? How have liberal values contributed (knowingly or unknowingly) to enshrining a white, male, straight, non-disabled, privileged-class power base? How do these affect minorities and disempower them? To break through systemic exclusion through solidarity and alliances, the privileged must grow in awareness of what is at stake in the struggle for justice, both for marginal groups and for themselves. We have to become accountable for all our privileges in an unequal landscape. If we subscribe to the view that God desires full life for all and invites us to work towards that end, then the capacity to realize the common good must exist as God will not require of us the impossible.

An urgent challenge before us ought to be work on the intersections of class, race, sex, gender, poverty, and its implications for belonging together. This is critical as these systems and the institutional interactions they reproduce heavily shape our moral-lives-in-relation. We can stop being an unwitting tool of inequality and become what some call a privilege traitor – deploying the power of our privilege as a tool for abundant life for all.

A significant act around our table space is that of remembering-recalling: how does remembering give agency to the multiplicity of experiences we embody? Where the agenda of empire causes a 'lack of bread' for many, power imbalances, and penury, will our 'remembering' reinforce boundaries that advance cultural, economic and spiritual superiority of one group or tradition over another? In the act of remembering, if we forget the power inequalities around the table (the explicit and implicit boundaries we work with), we may end up turning an intended inclusive space into one where some will be unable to find their voice or be reluctant to share the same space with those implicated as representing the dominant group (often keepers of the tradition).

In *The God of Small Things*, Arundhati Roy, through Chacko speaking to the twins, offers a helpful insight: Chacko explained to them that history (think tradition) was like an old house at night. With all the lamps lit and ancestors whispering inside: 'To understand history (or tradition),' Chacko said, 'we have to go inside and listen to what they're saying' (1997, p. 52). Belonging together entails a journey inside the tradition to listen, interrogate, unearth voices – especially the silenced ones in the process of arriving at what we have inherited as deposits of faith. Tradition is a dynamic process – always in formation, yet as Brian Gerrish writes (2003), 'There will always be a sharp difference between those who understand faithfulness to tradition as the preservation of past doctrines and those who understand it as recognizing that past ideas may be worthy of development.' My Reformed family understanding of the Church as *reformata et semper reformanda* is helpful here: the Church reformed, always reforming.

We are invited to join a challenging journey of critical scrutiny of the past (traditions). When texts of the past (our tradition) still continue to hegemonically form and inform contemporary ecclesial life, theology and practices, without any awareness of the culture-shaping world and structures in which they are steeped, it is time for intentional action. Awareness of how an 'oral and received tradition' evolved into a written one, and how exported and imported texts with their literary constructions and representations are already culturally and ideologically compromised, is necessary if tradition is not to become a tool for continuing exclusion.

Table Space: An Expansive Way

Around every corner in the Gospel narratives, we meet Jesus at a table, teaching and telling parables, making dramatic self-disclosures, gathering with his disciples, struggling to overcome barriers of hostility and division – living out generous, expansive love. Often it is at table with a host of 'dodgy' characters that we find Jesus living out God's offer of abundant life for all, working a different set of table-rules around a different economy. How does our life together reflect such generosity and expansive embrace? Can our belonging together be inclusive and gracious in order to embrace the range of diversity that we embody? Is there a limit? How can we avoid what starts out as and intends to be inclusive from becoming another means of exclusion?

Located in a complex liberal framework, I often wrestle with the ways liberal views can marginalize and exclude. Often our arguments around 'inclusion' (valid and well intentioned as they are) can lead us into a corner – a sort of 'zero sum game' – with one's vision of inclusion resulting in the exclusion of others. The politics of the liberal way, which gives agency to equality for all, will stand or fall on us believing and affirming that dehumanization anywhere and everywhere is wrong. The sad reality, though, is that even in the name of freedom, democratic values and equality, we can end up displaying a hierarchy in marginalization and oppression, much to the glee of the status quo. Perhaps we need to rediscover an original meaning of 'liberal' as 'free in bestowing, bountiful, overflowing, generous, expansive, open-hearted'.

'Expansive' is a helpful word – it allows us to be surprised by multiplicity and diversity in our belonging together around a common table. Being expansive suggests no privileging of one perspective over another but, rather, a critical engagement and conversation to catch a glimpse of the Divine. Being expansive is also helpful in enabling a dynamic engagement with a diverse 'cloud of witnesses' through our inherited texts and various traditions. Finally, being expansive means rediscovering the generous, open-hearted and recklessly extravagant grace of God in Christ. It also means renegotiating belonging, interrogating power and privilege, managing our complex identities and prejudices, and experiencing mutual inconveniencing. We cannot act inclusively out of the assumption that God's grace is limited and scarce. We have to rediscover the expansive heart of God in our ministry of inclusion.

Rowan Williams suggests that to participate in Holy Communion 'means to live as people who know that they are always guest' and that 'indiscriminate generosity and the willingness to mix with unsuitable people' were very much part of the life of the early Church (2014, pp. 41–2). Around the table space, we are all in need, and if belonging together is going to be truly expansive it means that space has to be renegotiated for all to be included. Because we are always guest and all in need, together we must be mutually inconvenienced for the sake of the economy of the host. Our God-talk and practices cannot be about reducing each other's perspective and practices – all must move out of their fear and comfort spaces into a grace-generosity space, even if it is costly and inconvenient.

This is the vision of an inter-cultural journey: moving beyond a mere recognition of the presence of a multiplicity of cultures or diversity with very little or no interaction beyond one's own group. Remaining in a place of minimal risk or interaction diminishes our common vocation together around the table of Christ. The invitation is for all of us to journey beyond our cultural/theological comfort/fear zones and boundaries to discover new insights of the Divine and what it means to be followers of the Jesus Way together, while allowing for multiplicity in the vision of togetherness. Together we enable each other to participate and experience inclusion by living out expansive habits characterized by 'mutual inconveniencing' (embracing each other's differences); courageously imagining new ways of being church so that the variety of 'giftings' are shared and received in ways that delight, enrich, renew and transform lives. Every time another joins us around the table, the way we are community has to be renegotiated to give agency to their presence.

Table Space: One in Christ and Identities

One of the Pauline notions associated with table space is the body of Christ as a basis for the ecclesial dimension of eucharist. Notions of 'body of Christ' and 'one in Christ' are not without an agenda. How do our theologies of the body of Christ shape our understanding of 'one in Christ'? Does our theological perspective allow room for the distinctiveness of identities and differences within the body? What does the collapsing (one in Christ) do to distinctive embodiment and how is this reflected in inclusion practices and belonging together? In contexts where identity plays a central role in the theological constructions of marginalized communities, how do we make sense of ethnic particularity within the Church's theological formulations? How do we re-read the interpretive tendencies of Paul's oneness theory that seems to subsume differences?

I wonder how much God-talk and liturgical practice honestly reflects the complexities of interaction and hybridity from the first Christian community to our current time. How much of our 'one in Christ' mantra unknowingly legitimizes a hegemonic unity that leaves little space for 'differences and diversity' by placing more emphasis on 'sameness of identity and 'unity'? In the debates and process meanderings in the United Reformed Church on same gender/sex marriage, underlying much of the debate was unity or 'one in Christ' mantra. The 'one in Christ' call may look like equality in the body. Closer scrutiny, however, will reveal that it carries an in-built threat to differences in the Christian economies of history – diminishing and restricting the existence of others. Because identity is a complex matter, the politics warrants analysis.

At the same time, an exclusive focus on identity politics with a pull towards looking inward may mean missing intersections or can lead to inaction. Because systemic transformation needs alliances, it will become necessary to include those outside of one's experience (of the minority group I may represent) – but who also embody similar (same) experiences – to interact and speak with and on my behalf. Identity does matter and paying attention to identity allows us to interrogate the process through which any dominant group have their opinions taken at face value, while minorities and non-normative groups of people struggle to have their voices heard. But we can also tire ourselves, totalize the complexities of identity, polarize our discourses, and can even internalize/re-inscribe some of the very habits we wish to counter when identity becomes our sole focus. To move to a politics of transformation and change, we need to grow and adjust our discourse. This requires effort and much grace.

Mystery, Silence and Imagining a Different World

The table space of Christ also operates in a different world/ economy (of the impossible). In the re-enacting, words are insufficient to embrace the mystery present. Whatever our theological colour: Protestant faith tends towards too much activism, premised on an unbalanced understanding of God as creator and *actus purus* (God as rester, no!). Is this why we invest little in developing and nurturing an interior life necessary to feed our activism? We do not know how to be silent/ to pause – as a countercultural act in a noisy world of orchestrated distractions. In favouring rationality, we can be suspicious of mystery – deducing and reasoning out every act of mystery, miracle, magic and grace. Mystery terrifies many of us. The mantra of 'growing in the faith' – meaning leaving behind childish things – can lead us to perceive Christians who subject their scriptures, liturgies and creeds to critical analysis as having a grown-up and mature faith. The others can then be located in the domain of an emotional, immature and childish faith. It is not impossible to see how this can lead to polarized perspectives – stifling inclusion. Belonging together means resisting and countering any tendency to 'pin down all meaning without anything that signifies mystery or risk' (Brueggemann 2000, pp. 2–5). Inclusive ministry can rediscover sacramental mystery and open up ways to re-imagine community in terms of in-between-space(s) and 'homelessness' around a common table. Fixed spaces, places and language fossilize and polarize identity and belonging, and 'remove any possibility of a genuine, open-ended engagement with others' or 'of seeing community in multiple contexts and through the lens of diversity' (Kim 2008, p. 37). Mystery, on the other hand, is that which displaces/unsettles, because there is more meaning than each of us around the table may be able to comprehend. Currently impoverished by an 'illiteracy of the imagination', we desperately need to find ways, beyond inclusion, to break through unhelpful polarizations, categories and restrictive habits to imagine a different world. We need fewer words to help us receive 'the gift of a new vision – the gift of seeing things' (Williams 2014, p. 52).

The Protestant obsession with words parcels out positions and truths in neat and precise words and language contrary to the Jesus way of ambiguity and fluidity. I find myself in an overly talkative ecclesial tradition: we talk about finances rather than releasing our grasp on the purse-strings for the sake of the

Jesus project of full life for all; we get aroused quarrelling about sex rather than enjoying it; we talk for days and months, reeling out reams of paper to justify our theological positions, assaulting God, when we could have broken out in poetry, music or just shut up to hear and catch a glimpse of the Divine. If, as Catherine Keller suggests, 'the church began in a mysterious transcultural event of amazement', where 'all were amazed and perplexed, saying to one another, "what does this mean? What has become of us?"' (Keller 2008, p. xi), what has the dominance of words, obsession with speech and proclamation and emphasis on a thinking/intellectual faith done to mystery?

Inclusion is not just a human endeavour. At the heart of Pope Francis' encyclical *Laudato Si'* is an integral ecology as a new paradigm of justice. The intersecting of perspectives (culture, economy, politics, social patterns, etc.) brings into play the ecology of our life together (including our institutions). Every dehumanizing and degrading act harms the whole. At the heart of our moving beyond inclusion is a plea for an integrated ecology, for we are faced with one complex crisis with multiple manifestations. Inclusion and belonging together does not happen when we malign or look down upon the capacity and ability of the 'other'; nor does it happen when two groups of people have the same idea, but it only becomes legitimate when the 'dominant voice' in the room offers it. We are not being inclusive when we refuse to interrogate our sacred deposits of faith for the seeds of exclusionary practices or when our leadership and key committees do not represent the variety of our membership; nor are we being inclusive when different opinions would be helpful, but different perspectives are not asked for, or are even dismissed and discounted. We are not including everyone when questions about who is absent from around the table are not asked or when conversations on the intersections of marginalization, privilege and power are missing. We are not including everyone when the narratives, images and language we use to describe our life together reinforce the dominant group and harmful stereotypes, and we are not being inclusive when we favour a talkative/reasoned faith at the expense of mystery/

silence. There is still much work to be done towards realizing communities of boundless, expansive compassion where none is excluded, but together we can find a way to belong together as a body of Christ in diversity and multiplicity.

Further Reading

Bhabha, H., 1994, *Location of Culture*, London & New York: Routledge.
Brueggemann, W., 2000, *Deep Memory, Exuberant Hope: Contested Truth in a Post-Christian World*, Minneapolis: Fortress Press.
Dirs, B., 2014, 'Does English Sport suffer from its Suspicion of Maverick Talent?', BBC Sport, http://www.bbc.co.uk/sport/0/cricket/25680571 (accessed 20.4.23).
Gerrish, Brian, 2003, 'Sovereign Grace: Is Reformed Theology Obsolete?', *Interpretation: A Journal of Bible and Theology*, 57(1), pp. 45–57.
Hanley, P., 2014, 'How we took our pick', *Church Times*, https://www.churchtimes.co.uk/articles/2014/26-september/features/features/how-we-took-our-pick (accessed 20.4.23).
Keller, C., 2008, *Mystery: Discerning God in Process*, Minneapolis: Fortress Press.
Kim, Yung-Suk, 2008, *Christ's Body in Corinth: the Politics of a Metaphor*, Minneapolis: Fortress Press.
Levine, A., 2007, *The Misunderstood Jew: The Church and the Scandal of the Jewish Jesus*, San Francisco: HarperOne.
Meyers, R., 2009, *Saving Jesus from the Church*, San Francisco: Harper One.
Rivera, M., 2007, *The Touch of Transcendence: A Postcolonial Theology of God*, Louisville & London: Westminster John Knox Press.
Roy, A., 1997, *The God of Small Things*, London: Flamingo.
Taylor, B. Brown, 2013 (first published 1998), *When God is Silent: Divine Language beyond Words*, Norwich: Canterbury Press.
Tkacz, N., 2015, *Wikipedia and the Politics of Openness*, Chicago: University of Chicago Press.
Williams, R., 2014, *Being Christian: Baptism, Bible, Eucharist, Prayer*, London: SPCK.

Note

1 This chapter is adapted from the author's 2015 Inclusive Church Annual Lecture.

3

Building Bridges

RUTH HUNT[1]

The Early Years

I'm not a theologian. I don't know my 'Greek translation of Leviticus and how it might conflict with the new translations of the second interpretation of ...', and so on, and so on. I'm not that person. I'm not the person who can necessarily provide every biblical rationale for the acceptance of LGBTQ+ people in the Church. I'm a campaigner, I'm an activist, and I'm a Christian, and it's from that perspective that I talk and write.

This chapter is about my history and my faith, and my journey with Stonewall and as a campaigner, and where I think we are today, as a society, as communities, in a world that feels increasingly fractured and fracturing. What is the role, more broadly, for inclusive Christianity, and how can we play a part in that? Sexual orientation and gender identity is an element of that, but it's an element that often becomes the canary in the coalmine for other dissatisfaction and division in our societies.

I was born in 1980 into a Catholic family – my parents and my extended family were very Catholic in a way that was quite natural for me. I was brought up in Wales. Wales is not a big Catholic country, but that probably is why my parents went for it. We absolutely had a normal, Catholic upbringing. We went to our local school and we went to our local church, and we were very much part of the community. As a child, as with a lot of children brought up in the Christian faith, that was our normal. We had our first communion, we had baptisms, my cousins all came through the schools, and the school was an absolute place of safety and security and moral values – a moral heart. In my day, in the 1980s and 90s, we didn't talk about sex very much, we certainly didn't talk about sexual orientation, but we did talk about love and respect and treating each other well.

When I reached 11 or 12, I started thinking about all sorts of matters of faith and I was a studious reader. By the age of 11, I'd probably read the Bible twice in school. I didn't know long division, but we certainly knew our Bible at our school. And by the age of 11, what I had been struck by was of course the story of Ruth (every child in the world goes to their own story) and the relationship between Ruth and Naomi, which I didn't then – and don't now – interpret as a same-sex relationship. What I do interpret it as is a story about a woman who goes against convention, in doing what she believed to be right – when society was asking her to do something different. The loyalty that Ruth demonstrates to Naomi moves me now and it moved me then.

My brother is called Thomas, and my parents were very clear that the reason they'd called him Thomas was because he was the one apostle who, when everybody was saying 'this is how it is', said 'I don't believe you. It's not how it is.' So, my parents, although hugely respectful of God in the Catholic tradition and the Catholic faith were very clear that Ruth and Tom both did something quite different. The narrative in our family was that Ruth and Tom had both done something quite different, and that was an important part of the story. It was not incongruous with one's faith to be different – it was absolutely in keeping with God's will that one should sometimes challenge the status quo and the authority around you.

When I was 12, I was beginning to realize that I was attracted to women – girls – but that didn't really have any impact on my faith whatsoever. What superseded that very big thought was the death of my aunt, when I was. She was 32 and died in childbirth. She had three little kids under the age of 5, and what happened at that key moment in an adolescent life is that those children came to live with us. We were part of a Catholic school and a Catholic community, and suddenly the church and the school wrapped themselves around us. Alongside the hymns and the Bible readings it all became profoundly important to me – and fancying girls didn't seem like a big deal. I certainly didn't question whether it was OK or not, bearing in mind I was at school during section 28, so there was no mention whatsoever of homosexuality in schools in any context.

At 14, I remember talking to my priest and saying 'Father, I think I'm attracted to girls not boys', and he said: 'The most important thing, kid, is to do your GCSEs, alright?' We might today have more guidance as to what a priest should say in these given moments – and perhaps he should have said more – but actually that's kind of what I needed to hear at the time. Get your head down, get on with your work, don't get too distracted. I think that was an incredibly important moment for me, where I'd obviously wound myself up for two years that this might be a problem, but then actually his words completely de-escalated the situation.

As I continued growing up, I studied English at A-Level and went on to study English at Oxford, and during all that time, age 13 to 18, I was reading Julian of Norwich, C. S. Lewis, the Bible – and still that rich, Christian tradition stayed very much a part of my discourse and dialogue and thinking. At Oxford, I studied everything from Beowulf to Virginia Woolf, but anything past Virginia Woolf was considered too modern and in fact anything not British was considered too modern. That said, you couldn't really get away from the influence of the Bible on English Literature. If you read Milton, you're reading the Bible, if you read Blake, you're reading the Bible.

At Oxford, I went back into the closet. A different closet. I didn't really talk about my faith at all, mainly because when you go to university – especially when you go to Oxford – you have to choose your tribe. I had very much chosen the gay tribe, and cathsoc was pretty hardcore at Oxford! So what I found myself doing is going to local parish churches. There was something quite comforting about going to family churches, rather than the hardcore, theological, Dominican-monk university approach. I didn't feel I was Catholic enough to be allowed into that space. I didn't feel like I could hold my own in that space, and I was also very 'out'. I was President of my college and President of the Student Union. I think I just closeted the faith bit instead, because it wasn't really something you talked about.

Building Bridges at Stonewall

After university, age 21 to 25, I lost God a bit, and I remember feeling incredibly angry that the organized Church and organized religion continued to say nothing about me. I think that the Catholic Church speaks great volumes about gay men, barely recognizes trans people, and lesbians just don't exist. That was about me understanding female sexuality and about the role of women in the Church. I remember behaving in a way which was 'unbecoming' for a Catholic girl, and feeling deeply sad, and thinking 'I can't believe God has forsaken me. Why would God leave me?' I had quite a profound realization that He hadn't left me – I'd left Him. But this realization came at a time when I thought that if I was going to be hung for being gay, I might as well do as much gay stuff as I could! To hell with the consequences – and the feelings of my partner! It wasn't until I matured later that I realized that this kind of attitude and approach to life was actually deeply uncomfortable for me and that it was undermining my values and my integrity, which is in fact where my faith comes from.

When I joined Stonewall in 2005, I was 25 and it was quite an interesting organization. In those days, we were 25 staff, and the turnover was about £1.7 million. Stonewall doesn't take any government funds at all, mainly because they were never offered. By 2018, we were probably closing in on a turnover of about £8 million, and we had 140 staff, so that gives you an idea of how much the organization has grown and changed. When I took over in 2014 as CEO, we were about half that size, so it's been growing and growing. In 2005, Stonewall was relentlessly pursuing what I would describe as an assimilation agenda. It was an agenda where we were 'as good as you'. With every organization, every institution we talked to, it was about making them feel better about the gay thing, whether that was politicians, employers, schools – it was all about presenting a very nice, neat idea of gay. I use the word gay purposefully as well, because Stonewall wasn't trans-inclusive in those days, it barely mentioned bisexuality at all, and I remember as a lesbian (I was a little baby dyke, no. 3 haircut, baggy jeans), I remember being really encouraged to, what I would describe as, 'femme up' to make myself a little bit more palatable to the men we were trying to influence, maybe start wearing brooches, you know! I encountered a huge number of people who tried to 'help me' on my way.

This went on for a good decade. When I became CEO in 2014, I was very clear that I didn't want to carry on the organization in that way. I think there is a way of both influencing establishment organizations and being able to acknowledge the complexity, the richness, the diversity of this LGBTQ+ community. I don't think that's incongruous. It's a bit of a stretch at times, I'll admit, but there is a possibility to keep these two things together. When I was deputy director of public affairs, I was on media phone and I took a call from one of the gay media outlets who said, 'We've heard that Soho is closing down its gay Catholic masses. Does Stonewall have a view?' and I said, 'Yes. Ruth Hunt, deputy director of public affairs, says that it's a real shame that they're closing down the Catholic masses, because it's really important.' And the journalist said, 'Do you know any gay Catholics?' and I said 'Yes, I'm a gay Catholic', because I was going to church and I was practising. Now, 'Deputy Director of Public Affairs is a Catholic' is not news, but 'CEO of Stonewall is Catholic' really is news. So, the first article when I became CEO, on the front page of the *Independent*, was 'Practising Catholic Takes Over Stonewall'.

That was a moment where I had quite a big decision to make. I had to decide whether I would talk about being Catholic, and about my faith in public, or whether I would say 'This is a private matter, I don't want to talk about it'. I went through what can only be described as an absolute crisis of confidence – 'I don't know the Greek translation of Leviticus', I thought 'and what if someone asks me about the Evangelical tradition and how it should be split from the Church of England and its influence on it? I don't know anything about that!' What I did know is that God is important, and God is Love and God is part of my life. I had a real anxiety about the questions people might ask about faith and theology. I then thought that I'm not Catholic enough to be able to talk about God and God is going to judge me for not being Catholic enough to be able to talk about God, because I'm not sure I want to believe in Him all the time, and my partner said 'If you're worried about what God thinks about that, you've probably passed the test of being Christian enough to talk about being Christian! If you're concerned that He might judge you for that, I think you're alright!' And that was good advice.

A wise man once said to me, 'Ruth, you're a campaigner and you're a communicator, and it is time that you use this opportunity and this role to talk about the role of faith in achieving social change, that you talk about your values and connect them to your faith, and that you try and find ways to make progress with faith communities' – and that's what I have chosen to do. I have tried to do that to the best of my ability. I did Greenbelt, and my poor atheist partner said, 'Why are we in a tent?! Why are we at a Christian festival in a tent?! This is not my idea of fun!' I have tried to answer the call when it is asked of me, but with a constant sense of inadequacy.

Stonewall tries to influence where it can. In 2018, we stood up to a small but increasingly vocal group of lesbian feminists who totally objected to trans inclusion. As a dyke running Stonewall, that was pretty tough. Your own tribe turning on you is pretty tough. We are strongly supportive of UK Black Pride, and I think that the way that other organizations have treated those who are working on UK Black Pride has been unacceptable, and Stonewall will always do everything in its power to support Black, Asian and minority ethnic LGBTQ+ people find their voices. If that means money, it will find money. And lo and behold, by calling out discrimination against Black people, by calling out discrimination against trans people, the volume of 'Stonewall has lost its way. It has no sense of mission. What about the gay men?' gets louder and louder. There are times when I think 'This is just really hard actually. It's really hard to push against boundaries when those boundaries are constantly coming back in and reinforcing themselves.' I think that the abuse that trans people are experiencing now is similar to the abuse we saw around HIV in the late 1980s, and it should be a wake-up call to all of us. The combination of some lesbians being angry about that, and some gay men being angry about Stonewall protecting Black people, and some people saying we shouldn't be doing God – there's no place for God in this – feels very indicative of where we are as a world right now.

I think we are a hurting community, and I find myself feeling increasingly hurt. I recently stopped going to my Catholic church and instead attended an inclusive church, and I feel like I'm taking an easy way out. That's a very Catholic response to God isn't it? I feel like I'm cheating. We all have to shake hands at the sign of the peace, which is way too extrovert for me. There's something very different about that space that I wanted to reject, because I don't feel worthy of it. I don't really feel like I'm allowed, I don't feel like I'm allowed to have a community, a pastoral faith community. I'm talking very frankly about my instincts. I sit there on a Sunday and think, 'Have I got to shake hands with everybody? Is somebody going to ask me about my week?' – because this never happens in a Catholic church. We don't even talk to each other in the Catholic Church! This could be cheating!

We are encouraged to not seek comfort and solidarity in each other in a society which is currently building walls. We are encouraged to fear each other, we are encouraged to believe that trans women have such complex narratives that they can't possibly be part of LGBTQ+. We're encouraged to think that the Church is our enemy, we're encouraged to believe that

Orthodox Judaism hates gay people so there's no point working with them. What's interesting about this polarization is that social media is no longer a reflection of it but is instead driving it. Social media used to be a barometer of it, and now it is creating hostility, creating division, and polarizing communities more than ever before. Stonewall works with a peace-building organization in the Sudan – to help us learn how to do non-violent communication between trans communities and radical feminist communities. These are the lengths we're going to in order to try and navigate this space, because the tendency to revert to hostility is really powerful at the moment.

For me personally, I believe that if we ever needed an explicit, vocal Christian faith, now is the time. I think that we desperately need to find different ways of talking to each other and building bridges, not walls. The thing that breaks my heart about the Church of England, for example, is that I think that the issue of the inclusion of LGBTQ+ people is a proxy for a bigger discussion. I don't think it's really just about just LGBTQ+ issues, and I find its weakness unforgiveable and frustrating. Catholics are just a mess of contradiction. Catholics have always been a mess of contradiction. The sooner the Vatican gets a gay network group, the better! Then we can actually start making some progress! The Church of England should be better than this. It's how the denomination works. The Church of England should be able to cope with dissent and disagreement – good disagreement. I spoke to Synod in 2017. I was slightly undercover; in that I didn't tell Stonewall I was doing it. And I thought 'This suits you. This indecisiveness suits how you work.' And the Church of England needs to be better than that.

I haven't got many easy answers, except that I keep praying to give strength to Stonewall and other organizations to keep standing up to those who oppose trans people, and the people in the gay community who seem to think that it's acceptable to be racist. Stonewall will keep standing up to those who say, in the name of God, that there is no place for lesbian, gay, bisexual and trans people, because it's simply not true. It has never sat comfortably with me, even when I was in a time of crisis. But we need to be louder, and I think that the time for polite dissent and disagreement is passing. I think we should be angry about the way in which people are excluded from our communities, and I think that we should find a way to express that anger with love and respect. This exclusion should not be done in the name of Jesus, and it should not be done in the name of God, and I will continue in my amateurish, slightly clumsy way to do my best to speak truth to power. And I hope that anything Stonewall can do to support you, it will do, and anything you can do to support Stonewall, it will embrace.

Note

1 This chapter is based on the Inclusive Church Annual Lecture Ruth gave in 2018.

4

Poverty Has a Woman's Face

LORETTA MINGHELLA[1]

Does Poverty Have a Woman's Face?

Christian Aid's experiences of working with people in poverty have demonstrated that at every level, from the household to the global stage, in politics and in personal life, in economics and in health, in culture and in decision making, people of one gender are poorer, disadvantaged and less powerful than another. For that reason, Christian Aid often says that yes, sadly poverty does have a woman's face.

At the time of writing this, around 700 million people live below the global poverty line, on less than a $1.90 day. They will go to bed hungry. It's been estimated that around 70% of these people, over two-thirds of the world's extreme poor, are women and girls. Women represent half the world's population, perform nearly two-thirds of its work hours, receive 10% of the world's income and own less than 1% of the world's property. Women's wages worldwide are 17% lower than those of men. And those jobs they do have are more likely to be low-paid, low-status and vulnerable jobs, with limited or no social protection or basic rights. Globally, only 18% of chief executives are women. In the UK, despite being half a century down the line from the Equal Pay Act, women are still paid 17.5% less than men.[2] As we here face this reality, we know that we, as people of faith, as believers in the one body, must work for the transformation of global society, so that the world becomes an inclusive place where women and men may flourish and live in peace with one another.

My own personal and professional experience is itself a story about gender, so allow me to share a little of that. When I was young, the idea that I could ever become the CEO of a large international development organization would have been thought of as little more than an idle fantasy. I was born into an Italian family with all the accompanying pressures you might expect in 1960s Britain. In the Isle of Wight, being Italian was something out of the ordinary, and coming from an ice-cream-making family a little bit exotic – certainly not the standard for aspiring to any serious role. My first job was as a pre-schooler turning the jingle on and off on my dad's ice cream van. When, at 14, I told the school careers advisor I wanted to be a barrister, or possibly a diplomat, I was told that both would probably be too difficult, and anyway I wasn't English enough for the second. I was told I should pursue speech therapy, in the light of what was then a national shortage.

My career aspirations were unusual for a young girl of Italian origins, who might have been expected to concentrate on finding a nice Italian boy to settle down with. One of the men in my extended family, on hearing me express some rather forthright views about business as a young teenager, advised me in no uncertain terms that because I was a girl, having a view on anything much was not welcome, that I should concentrate on trying to make myself less physically unattractive, and that if I didn't keep myself to myself I would never get a husband. Luckily my parents were really keen to support my ambitions and, after a law degree at university, I qualified as a solicitor, despite having to field illegal questions from some law firms along the way about whether there was any point in investing in my training if I was only going to have children. I moved from legal practice into financial regulation – both male-dominated environments. When I eventually arrived as CEO at Christian Aid, I even found that the charity sector at senior levels is still dominated by men.

However, I ended up in one of the most amazing roles you

could hope for – leading an organization of over 900 staff with over 600 partner organizations in over 30 countries committed to ending global poverty, including the gender inequality that helps to drive it. Very soon my daughter is about to start her legal training and you can be assured that no one asked her an illegal question when she went for her solicitor's training contract, and no career advisor suggested her choice was beyond her, nor did any family member suggest that she should concentrate on landing a husband. Neither she nor I have progressed on our own. We stand on the shoulders of many brave people, mainly but not exclusively women, who have battled to make it possible for women like us to have aspirations which even a generation before us would have been unrealistic – and we have depended on the encouragement of so many others all along the way.

Of course, even in Britain, gender equality is still not a reality, but progress has been made. Together we have all achieved so much. But here and across the world, there is so much more to do. The facts and figures that I shared with you earlier could fool us into believing that inequality is about money and hence we can buy our way out of it: just enough aid, just enough donations. But we can't. For although in the developing world a woman dies every 90 seconds as a result of childbirth, this is not simply for lack of health facilities, it is because a woman's ability to access reproductive health services depends not primarily on the existence of the service, but on whether her husband will allow her to control her own body, use contraception and travel to a family planning clinic. We know that the same girl who is forced into an early marriage is the same girl who will be forced into a lifetime of unpaid domestic labour, who will not be given the opportunity of going to school, who may be forced to have her genitals mutilated and, when her husband finally dies, will be denied the right to inherit any property. For many it is a form of slavery for which the dawn of emancipation, from birth to death, hardly even flickers.

For Christian Aid, ending gender inequality (and indeed all forms of poverty) is not about the numbers of schools or clinics built, it is about redressing fundamental imbalances of power. It is about giving people in poverty, and especially women, a voice, choice and control over their own lives, because, as a Christian organization, we believe that each person is made in the image of God. Every person, irrespective of race, creed, colour, gender or sexuality, is a person of inherent dignity and infinite worth.

> So God created humankind in his image,
>   in the image of God he created them;
>   male and female he created them.
>
> (Genesis 1.27)

This verse offers a picture of humankind being created as the last part of God's creation, and, most significantly, not simply 'after its own kind' or like itself, but made in the image of God. What this 'being in the image of God' precisely implies is not explained. This verse should perhaps be read in the context of those many verses in the Old Testament that stress to us that God cannot be looked at, nor can we know what God looks like.

It is striking that it is both male and female together who are described as being 'in the image of God', so that no one human being can be this 'image' alone – there is a ready-made protection against idolatry. But it is astonishingly difficult for those who read this verse often, and for whom it has become almost a kind of slogan, to feel today quite the force and ground-shaking impact that it must have had in its original context. There were societies in the ancient Near East, like the Babylonians, who believed that not all that exists was good, and that some things that existed were actually bad. Against that background, this verse, which seems now almost blandly obvious to us, was profoundly significant. This whole account of creation in the first chapter of Genesis emphasizes right from the beginning that God made everything, and that it was all good. God made the light, and God made the darkness too. God made the land, and God made the water. And, significantly in terms of a theology of gender, God made male and female, and both are good. This was such an unusual and astonishing idea for the ancient world, and perhaps still sometimes today, that its full significance is hard to grasp.

The second account of creation, the one often presented as the story of Adam and Eve, has a similarly significant message. In Genesis 2 we read how the Lord God formed a human being from the dust of the ground and breathed into his (or, better at this stage, 'its') nostrils the breath of life. Then, further on in the story, we read that God decided it was not good for the creature to be alone. When the human being could not find anyone from among the animals or the birds to be a companion, God took one of the creature's ribs and made another human being and they were 'one flesh'. What is much clearer in the original Hebrew language in which this story is written is that the first creature that God made was simply an 'earthling' (this is what Adam means in Hebrew, a creature from the earth). It is only when the second creature is made, when the first one is divided to make two, that new words for 'man' and 'woman' are used. The very significant thing about this passage for a theology of gender is the way in which the relationship between the now differentiated 'man' and 'woman' is described. The earthling needs to find relationship and someone to heal loneliness. None of the creatures already made will do. So God makes the earthling into two, and yet two who are so completely of the same being that the earth creature can say, 'This at last is bone of my bones and flesh of my flesh'.

The message of the story is not that woman was derived from man or that woman is secondary, or even really that woman is so 'different' from man. What the text wants the reader to understand is that woman and man, female and male, are more like each other than they are different. They have a deep and essential unity with one another, being from the same source. They have something like common ground, the kind of unity that gives them a deep-rooted equality of dignity and worth.

Jesus and Gender Justice

A further source of reflection on gender, just as radical and transformative as those key texts in the book of Genesis, comes in Jesus himself. The Gospels bear witness to a Jesus who lived out an alternative masculinity and related to women in ways that absolutely embodied the joy and justice of our creation as 'male and female' – both in the image of God. Jesus lived in a context in which human beings exercised power over others in a multitude of ways. Divisions ran deep between Gentile and Jew, between Jew and Samaritan, between slaves and owners, between ruling Romans and subject peoples. There were multiple causes of discrimination, oppression and injustice, and many intersecting identities. But in each particular culture it was the case that men held power over women.

We see this reflected in the Gospel narratives, in which women are often unnamed, are silent and voiceless, or cast either as wives or prostitutes. But Jesus subverted and challenged the 'default' gender narrative. It is clear in the Gospels that Jesus often seems to go to the places where women are. There are women among his closest friends, and he speaks to women in public even though this is seen as improper behaviour. He acknowledges that women can be prophetic, and encourages Mary, the sister of Martha, to listen to his teaching in a way traditionally reserved for male disciples. He heals women and gives them dignity. If the world told women to be silent, it's Jesus who entrusts them with the task of proclaiming the resurrection.

Jesus also emerges from the pages of the Gospels as a remarkable kind of man, subverting traditional understandings of masculinity. This is really important in the way we work with men and with boys. He weeps, for his friends and for his community. He rejects the path of retaliative violence. After he is betrayed, he is neither assertive nor vocal, but silent-passive and yet unafraid. In John's Gospel, Pilate says to the people as Jesus is presented to them for mockery, 'Here is the man!' If any of us need new 'gender models', if gender justice can only come as masculinity is itself renewed, if boys and men need to rediscover gender as something personally challenging and transforming, then Jesus is 'the man'. This is the context in which we can make sense of what Paul says when he writes, 'There is no longer Jew or Greek, there is no longer slave or free, there is no longer male and female; for all of you are one in Christ Jesus' (Galatians 3.28).

At the heart of our faith is a belief in equality. The all-encompassing love of Christ is so vast and deep that it overlooks our differences and brings us all together as one. So, with the example of Jesus in our minds, if we are serious about tackling poverty we have to tackle gender inequality. The work of Christian Aid teaches us very clearly that poverty is not just about money. Poverty is about the uneven distribution of personal, social and political as well as economic power. And women are worse off, the world over, in each of these dimensions. Let's focus on those four dimensions, starting with the lack of personal power, which manifests itself in physical vulnerability. One of the things that has horrified me most in my travels around the world is the extreme physical vulnerability which women face.

Violence

Domestic violence and sexual violence against women are major public health problems. Global prevalence figures from the World Health Organization indicate that 35% of women worldwide have experienced either intimate-partner violence or non-partner sexual violence in their lifetime. On average, 30% of women who have been in a relationship report that they have experienced some form of physical or sexual violence by their partner.[3] In 2013, UN research based on 10k men in Asia found that one in four admitted to have committed a rape, sexual entitlement being the main reason – the belief that men are entitled to sex regardless of consent. Rape is often used as a weapon of war and there is evidence that it rises after natural disasters. I remember the shock of hearing, for example, when we were working in Haiti after the earthquake in 2010, that women in the camps reported wearing several pairs of jeans because they were at risk of being raped in their tents. Wearing several pairs of jeans helped buy them time to raise the alarm if they were attacked.

Family Planning

Now add that more than 220 million women in developing countries have great difficulty in accessing family planning. Inadequate family planning when combined with inadequate maternal healthcare means that pregnancies happen earlier and more frequently than is safely managed. Young girls often become pregnant as soon as they start ovulating and long before their bodies are ready. In 2015, there were around 303,000 maternal deaths globally, almost all of them in developing countries.

Social Power Dimension

Moving on beyond the purely personal power dimension to the social dimension, women's place in society is not guaranteed before the law. In still too many countries (for example, the Democratic Republic of Congo, Yemen, Sudan) women are prevented from doing certain kinds of jobs and/or have to ask permission from their husbands to embark on a profession or open a business. In many countries, daughters and sons do not have equal inheritance rights. Many countries fail to outlaw domestic and sexual violence. In practice, national laws even where they exist are not enforced. In many parts of the world, customary laws and family codes which are discriminatory take precedence over national legislation. So, whatever the position at the national level on marrying off a girl of 12 to a 60-year-old man, or FGM, or honour killing, it may not be outlawed in the traditional legal system enforced where that girl lives. It remains a matter of sorrow and condolence in many countries when a woman gives birth to a girl rather than a boy, and the statistics show that the preference for a son in some countries does not just entail a series of commiserations. According to the 2011 census in India, there were 927 girls for every 1,000 boys in 2001, and that ratio is actually getting worse – there were only 919 girls for every 1,000 boys in 2011. Gender-based terminations have played a part in this.

The Political Dimension

Women are underrepresented at every level of decision-making, which affects them in the political realm right across the world. Only 22% of all national parliamentarians across the world were female as of January 2015. I won't dwell on that because it won't surprise you: we're all too familiar with that here in the UK. In 2016, only 29% of the House of Commons were female and only 25% of the House of Lords.

The Economic Dimension

I've already touched on this, but it's worth spelling out that it's more than an issue of equal pay. Let me say something about tax. We've heard a lot recently about how tax dodging is diminishing public revenues and disproportionately impacts poor people. This is acutely true in poor countries where essential public services like maternal health care are so woefully underfunded. Developing countries often find it difficult to raise sufficient revenues because of widespread tax dodging by multinational corporations and wealthy individuals. The IMF has routinely advised such countries to look to VAT as an income generator; it is efficient, raises a considerable amount of revenue and is relatively easy to administer. It is unsurprising, then, that in developing countries, income from VAT can represent a substantial proportion of total tax revenue – often around a quarter. In 2013, the Kenyan government amended the VAT laws to impose VAT on a long list of essential household items. This change had a much greater impact on the disposable income of women, because many of these items were on the list of what women rather than men are expected to buy. In April 2014, following a campaign led by civil society, including Christian Aid's partners, the Kenyan government passed an amendment to the VAT bill to reinstate VAT exemptions for many of these items including fertilizers and staple foods.

Another brake on women's economic power is the huge burden of unpaid domestic work. A recent project of ours in Ethiopia was typical in identifying that a woman's day involved about 18 hours of work, mostly unpaid, whereas a man did about 7 hours' work, mostly paid. Unpaid women's work commonly involves walking miles to collect water and firewood. Because of this burden of work, many girls are not encouraged to complete their education, but rather to help their mothers at home. No wonder a girl in South Sudan is more likely to die in childbirth than to finish school. Uneducated girls are less likely to get well-paid work or become politically active. And so the cycle continues.

Climate and Gender

Across all four dimensions then – personal, social, political and economic power – women are discriminated against: and one dimension of poverty feeds another. You see this come together when you look at the implications of climate change for women and girls. Climate change affects women and girls more harshly, because women are more vulnerable to the floods, droughts and diseases that are expected to increase as the climate changes. Climate change's gender discrimination will be far more pronounced in those swathes of the poorer, developing world where sexual inequality is typically much greater, where the effects of global warming will be more extreme, and where less money is available to protect against the consequences. Women in poorer countries tend to be more vulnerable because, when disaster strikes, they are far more likely to be in the home cooking, cleaning or looking after others, putting them at greater risk from collapsing buildings.

That is just one of many reasons why women tend to suffer disproportionately in natural disasters in the developing world. Research suggests that women could be considered more vulnerable in severe storms because they are less likely to have been taught to swim in poorer countries, as well as being less likely to own a mobile phone which could be used to call for help. In the most extreme cases of disasters in patriarchal societies, women may be unable to leave the house without a male companion or their movement can even be hampered by long clothing. Of the 150,000 people killed in the 1991 Bangladesh cyclone, 90% were women and you see similar disproportionate impacts on women in the tsunami of 2005 as well.

Not only do women typically suffer more than men in the kind of climate-related disasters likely to result from global warming – they are also far more vulnerable to the day-to-day impact of rising temperatures. They are more exposed to the mosquito-borne diseases such as malaria, dengue and chikungunya, which they come into contact with through the duties of water collection and food harvesting that typically fall to women, and which are transmitted through floods and rising humidity. Women are also more likely to go without food in the event of food shortages because of drought, while water scarcity means they sometimes have to travel huge distances to collect water. This task will become more difficult and require longer walking distances, which may heighten the risk of women and girls being assaulted. Most importantly, it robs them of precious time which they could dedicate to education. If political leaders around the world are serious about poverty, if they're serious about gender equality, they must also get serious about climate change.

Solutions

Thankfully there are solutions. In the UN Sustainable Development Goals,[4] goal number 5 focuses on gender equality – a standalone goal for gender equality. This means that all the other goals aren't met if they're not met for women. Also, pressing for legal change is extremely important; we must press for laws everywhere that guarantee equal pay and equal rights to inherit, and that outlaw child marriage, FGM and domestic abuse. Another important step is to work with men and boys to change the harmful social norms. Men and boys are diminished by the diminishing of women and girls. Our models of masculinity are very damaging for men and boys too. To help kickstart the necessary shifts in cultural understanding, Christian Aid often starts by getting men and women to talk to one another. If women find it hard to be good partners, mothers, daughters, sisters and citizens, men also struggle to be good partners, fathers, brothers, sons and citizens too, and to live up to those expectations society puts upon them. Christian Aid and its partner organizations get them to talk frankly about these pressures and share them. We are all, often unwillingly, pigeon-holed into roles and expectations of behaviour and emotion set from birth. We are all, as individuals, both part of the problem and part of the solution.

At the community level, Christian Aid helps women build secure livelihoods, to organize and seek political space, stand up for their rights, and access education and decent community health care. But the work to end gender inequality from Brazil to Bangladesh is, at its heart, about tackling relationships between those with power and those without. We recognize that faith leaders hold great power to foster compassion and positive change within a community. Over the past 70 years Christian Aid has often partnered with faith leaders, particularly on work to combat HIV and HIV stigma, but faith leaders are by no means the silver bullet or always the right choice, as they can too often be complicit in reproducing harmful practices and attitudes. However, Christian Aid is seeking to change that. In March 2015, a number of faith-based organizations and institutions were invited to a consultative workshop to discuss ways of addressing gender injustice. The outcome was the decision to establish a movement of people of faith who will work together to bring about change and create justice and equality for all people, regardless of gender. A global inception group began planning, and Side by Side[5] was born – the product of much collaboration. Side by Side recognizes that gender justice cannot be achieved by individual efforts alone. It therefore works to build a more coordinated and collaborative faith movement which:

- Builds greater awareness amongst people of faith, faith leaders and institutions of the moral and theological imperative for gender justice, and supports them to demand this of themselves, their own partners, communities and leaders.
- Establishes safe spaces for senior faith leaders and champions of gender justice to discuss, understand and commit to take leadership action on gender justice at every level from the household to global.
- Builds the capacity of faith actors to challenge and change harmful social, religious and cultural norms and to implement practical activities to address gender injustice.

Conclusion

I started by saying that 50 years ago it would have been thought an idle fantasy to imagine that I would become the female CEO of an international development organization. When I visited Christian Aid's programme in Bangladesh in 2012, I stood in front of 200 incredible women who had together worked and planned and collaborated to rebuild their community after Cyclone Aila, and their lead spokeswoman nearly couldn't speak when she stood up to make her presentation. Then she said, 'I'm sorry, it's just that I never imagined I would be standing here talking to someone like you'. I said, 'It's ok; I never imagined I'd be here either'. It's that sense of shifting power which moves me and gets me excited. It's the change we all want to see, and it's the change that, in a way which wasn't really possible before, we can now be a part of. I'd like to ask you all now reading this how you could help secure gender justice for the world's poorest women and girls. Whether it's local, national or global change we're looking for, it starts with us. It is through the good will and involvement of individuals like you that we can collectively make a difference in our world.

If I had to give an answer to the question 'Does poverty have a woman's face?', it would be abundantly clear from the examples above that that answer is yes. Numerically it is a discrimination that affects so many. However, *all* groups marginalized by identity – whether that is race, belief, disability, sexuality or gender identity – suffer disproportionately from poverty. Poverty is about the misdistribution of power, of injustice unredressed by love. It mars the image of God in each one of us. It takes from us the place at the table which Jesus laid for each one of us as equals. Do you dare to dream? I do. It might be interesting to imagine how different the world would be if everyone actually believed that, though we are all different, we all matter equally and are all irreplaceable.

On the front of Christian Aid's strategy document Partnership for Change, there are the soaring words from Psalm 99.4 – 'lover of justice, you have established equity'! From that notion of equity – that we, whilst different, are all equal because we are all made in the image of God – from that notion flows the joy, the energy and the purpose of Christian Aid's work. Once we realize this truth – that we are all equal, irreplaceable, uniquely beautiful – we, as people of Christian faith, but also those of other faiths and none, can rally together to love our global neighbours as the uniquely beautiful and worthy people that they are. Let's work together towards a world where poverty no longer has a woman's face or indeed any face at all.

Notes

1 This chapter is based on Loretta Minghella's 2016 Inclusive Church Annual Lecture.
2 As Loretta gave this annual lecture in 2016, the stats may have changed slightly since. Updated figures are on the Christian Aid website and in UN documents online. Loretta's points all still hold true.
3 As above, updated figures would be easy to find on the Christian Aid website and on UN documents online.
4 http://www.un.org/sustainabledevelopment/sustainable-development-goals (accessed 13.5.23).
5 https://www.christianaid.org.uk/get-involved/get-involved-locally/scotland/side-side (accessed 13.5.23).

5

Dismantling Whiteness and Deconstructing Mission Christianity

ANTHONY REDDIE[1]

Dismantling Whiteness

In this chapter, I want to highlight two ongoing conversations that I have been thinking about for the last 35–40 years. It is a strange experience finding yourself having thought about issues for so long which, for the most part, white Christians have completely ignored – until an African American man called George Floyd was murdered. Suddenly, it's as if the broader sweep of Christendom catches up with what some of us have been talking about for a long time.

First, I want to enflesh this notion of whiteness. It's not necessarily about white people. It's about a way of being in the world. A lot of this work owes a great deal to the great Willie James Jennings, an African American post-colonial scholar. In 2009, he published a brilliant book called *The Christian Imagination*. He followed this up with *After Whiteness*. In both books, what Jennings does is to begin to think constructively about the way in which this phenomenon of whiteness has captured our imagination and not in a good way. It is a construct that has been very hierarchical and has dominated the narrative on what it is to be human for a very long time. Christianity, which was supposed to be different, has been captured along with it. Part of the corrosiveness and toxicity of whiteness is that it is so normalized that we don't see it. It has become almost self-evident that this is what it is to be human.

It took the murder of George Floyd to change this. Sadly, African American people and people of African descent have been murdered in this way for a very long time, but this time it was caught on camera. Something about being caught on camera created a visceral response in a way that had not been the case for any of the millions of murders that had happened – going back to the experience of slavery.

Where does this all start for me? I have a northern accent – I've lived for 36 years in Birmingham, but I've never lost my Yorkshire accent. I still sound how I did in 1984, when I came to Birmingham for university. Before this, I was at Tong Comprehensive school in Bradford. It was more a zoo than a school. I was part of a small group of bookish nerds. I was doing A-Level English. Literature was my first love before I did a degree in History. One day, my English teacher comes up to me and says, 'Anthony, I've come across a book I think you would be interested in. A really important book.' He gives me a copy of *Things Fall Apart* by Chinua Achebe. It's one of the first great African novels, published in 1958. Achebe is writing about a changing South Africa in the 1950s. Modernity and what we now call post-colonialism is beginning to change African society. The teacher said, 'This is an important book for you to read.' There were only two Black people in our class – me and a young woman. I remember thinking, 'Why is it important for me to read but not for the rest of the class to read?' I quickly deduced that it was important for me because it was a book by an African and I was a Black person.

At the same time, when doing A-Level English, we were studying a Jane Austen book for the course – I think it was *Emma*. I have to say that I hated Jane Austen. Here was a book that said nothing and meant nothing to me. Why is it that only I had to read Chinua Achebe, but everyone in the class had to read Jane Austen? I thought, 'What makes Jane Austen universal and Chinua Achebe particular?' When Jane Austen was writing her book, I'm pretty sure she didn't have me or anyone like me in mind. Age 17, I didn't have the intellectual apparatus to say this, but it hit me that some people's contexts could be construed as universal and other people's as particular to them. Austen is writing about a particular time and milieu – provincial England at the time of the slave trade on the cusp of the industrial revolution. She is a great observer of social manners and my antipathy towards her has softened over the years. She could tell a good tale! However, I'm still scarred by having to read and re-read *Emma*. I still blame Jane Austen entirely for the fact that I did so badly in my A-Level English! I then abandoned English and went into History instead.

Since that moment, I have had this question in my mind – why are some people universal and some particular? I then went on to study theology at the University of Birmingham. I remember one of the tutors asking us to read Karl Barth. I've come to dislike Barth even more than I ever disliked Jane Austen. It was clear to us that this was someone who transcended the social contexts in which he wrote in order to speak universal truth – everyone had to read this irrespective of the contexts they were in. Around this time, I came across Robert Beckford, and through him I came across the work of James Cone. Cone then changed my life. I still find it interesting that Cone was only on this discreet extra course being taught by Robert Beckford. He wasn't on the general curriculum that everyone had to follow and engage in. I only found out about Cone because I came in from outside to study this course – I wasn't studying at the Queen's Foundation, where Beckford was teaching, but joined in with this course on a Tuesday afternoon, which he was running for people who had an interest. Cone was just part of a very discreet course for Black students. Of course, there was nothing that had universal application. It was just for Black people.

I'm now older and wiser and know this is not true. I remember having a conversation with a tutor at Queen's in which I asked why Cone wasn't on the curriculum for everyone to study. He said something along the lines of 'Well, Cone has important things to say about racism, but his work lacks universal application for all people'. This seemed a bit rich, when you consider that Queen's is set in a very wealthy area in Birmingham, and – at the time – it wasn't uncommon for Black people to be stopped by police officers and asked what they were doing, just because they were walking in the area. They stopped us simply because they thought somehow that we should only be living in Handsworth or Balsall Heath and never in Edgbaston or Harborne. It is somewhat ironic that someone could be stopped on racist presumptions, but James Cone had nothing to say to white society.

From those two encounters, I've found myself for the last 25 years thinking about these questions. Why are some people universal and some people marginalized and particular? They are good to read, but not for everyone. They are never compulsory on a curriculum. This is because whiteness has become the definition of what is construed as true. We are really talking of white, cis men of Empire. These are the people who have created the conceptual norms. It is a way of mastering control, of being able to define the world with you at the centre. It never names this. It is a way of seeing and being in the world, but it is not named. We are all caught up in it. Jennings says something like this: 'Imagine that all of us are fish in the sea. The sea becomes what is normal to us. Actually, the only time you realize there's something odd about your existence is if you're taken out of the sea and pulled into the air. While you're in the sea and you're a fish, you don't give it a second thought. That is how whiteness operates.'

It is so normative that most people don't even see it. We name things only if they are particular and 'other'. We have post-colonial theology, Black theology, but we never name whiteness. I want to reply to people who ask what I do: 'I teach theology'. What kind of theology? Oh, just theology. Because white theology is just called theology. Why can I not say that I am just teaching theology? Jane Austen is never considered a white writer. She might be called a female writer, even a feminist writer, but her whiteness is not important; it is never mentioned. The thing that is not mentioned is just the norm. It is the thing against which everything else is defined. It becomes the template by which we judge everything else.

I remember watching a documentary many years ago by one of the first critics of race, called Paul Gilroy, who, in his first book *There Ain't No Black in the Union Jack* (1982), was the first to outline the way in which Britishness and Englishness was predicated on a form of tacit whiteness. It still exists. If you want to understand how three Black footballers can get booed and get hate mail for missing some penalties, you need to understand that what belonging looks like is a white skin. Belonging and a sense of acceptability is framed around whiteness, because that's the historical norm on which colonialism and Empire was constructed. Gilmore gives this example – I believe it was Gilmore – of going into a shop and asking for a plaster and they have 'skin coloured' plasters. Whose skin is it? It never says 'white people's skin'; it just says 'skin coloured'. It says this is for the people with the skin colour of the people who matter in the world, even though most people in the world are not white.

When we're thinking about deconstructing and decolonizing the curricula, the first thing we need to do is name whiteness. At the very least, we need to challenge and recognize the fact that this phenomenon has created the norms, formed the world, and shaped people's understandings. When I was around 11, in the Methodist church where I grew up, I would be with the other children in the far room, so we could be as noisy and mischievous as we liked and not upset the nice, polite, middle-class people of the church. In that Sunday School room, there was a picture of Jesus – a Jesus who looked more like Bjorn Borg than Bjorn Borg himself. This was a blond-haired, Nordic-looking Jesus. This didn't resemble the real Jesus who lived in first-century Palestine, but it didn't matter. It was the Jesus of Empire. Whiteness creates God in its own image. It has no basis in historical fact, but that's not the point. The central doctrines of Christianity are in the image of whiteness. It is a reflection of the particular privilege of whiteness. Wherever you went in the room, the eyes would be watching you. The teacher would tell you Jesus was watching you if she had to leave the room! At the time, I remember thinking to myself, 'Who am I, in relation to this Jesus?'

One day, I summoned up the courage and asked my Sunday School teacher, 'If that is Jesus, and we are all made in the image of God, who am I?' She said, 'It doesn't matter'. In one way, she was right. It was a church which was very loving, and my mother brought me up with the knowledge that God loved me and everyone else. But on another level, it was a problem. We had very few images in the church, but those that did exist did not look like people like me. I finally saw a picture of a Jesus who was not white in my late twenties. When I graduated from the middle group at Sunday School into the senior group, I was given a copy of *The Illustrated Bible*, in which all the characters were depicted as white apart from the devil in the story of Jesus' temptation in the wilderness – the devil was depicted as Black.

Deconstructing Mission Christianity

We have to name whiteness, but we have to do more than that; we have to deconstruct it. There is nothing wrong with a white Jesus, as long as it sits alongside other images of Jesus. There is nothing wrong per se with Jane Austen. I have come to enjoy all the adaptations of her books on TV. But here's the thing, in terms of how we think about deconstructing Mission Christianity: we have to accept that whiteness has been conjoined with how we think about the Christian faith. This form of Christianity is not neutral. It is dangerous. It's dangerous because of what it propagates. It propagates power and imperialism. It propagates top-down notions of being. It's the way in which we still have a framing of our faith in which, when we think about what God is like, God is represented in the image of cis, white men. The reason why our churches struggle to be inclusive is because what we have imbibed is not the gospel, as reflected through the experiences of a Palestinian Jew who is othered in his own context; it is reflective of Empire. It's reflective of the people who control the narrative. Cis white men get to control what God is like and get to create doctrines which they say are universal – doctrines which somehow never impact upon them but always impact upon the 'other'. Therefore, part of the whole decolonizing process has to be to challenge and critique what we see as normative.

Doctrines have been fossilized for us for over 2,000 years, but any cursory reading of church history – which is interesting because I hated my first degree in church history and was a terrible undergraduate – reveals that they are formed as much as political arguments as they are by any so-called movement of the Holy Spirit. Yet so many of our churches hold onto them, because what they want to hold onto is a framework which puts people in their appropriate place, where some bodies are acceptable and some bodies are transgressive, and others we simply don't want to talk about. That's the impact of whiteness.

I have seen a great number of times that our processes in the Church are largely a form of socialization to get certain bodies to conform to a framework of authority that insists on who can belong and who can't. I still remember sitting on a selection panel about 25 years ago, looking at candidates who were offering for ministry. There are two things I remember from that panel. First, there was a man who had a double first from Cambridge, who was a practising solicitor and pretty much a functioning atheist. When we asked him a question like 'Can you explain your call?', he was very clever in being able to deconstruct the question without ever really answering it. 'What is a call?', he'd say. 'Well, that's an interesting question, isn't it? In philosophical, ontological and epistemological terms, calls can be understood in a variety of ways.' He went on like that throughout the interview. I remember thinking, 'Who is this person? Why does he want to be a Methodist minister? He doesn't seem to believe in anything.' At the end of the interview, the committee said, 'Wow. Isn't he such an eloquent individual?' So we accepted him. To quote one person present, 'Wouldn't it be such an asset for the Methodist Church to have someone like him?' Part of the power of whiteness is that there is a norm of not just whiteness, but of cis, white men from Oxbridge. It's a kind of respectability politics, where what we want is for our ministers to be somehow au fait with the powers that be, with the central establishment. If you talk to ministers who were ordained 40 years ago, they will tell you that there was a time when there were elocution lessons for working-class people, because if you were going to be clergy, and therefore part of the ruling class, you had to sound a particular way.

So this guy sails through, because he fits the typology of what we expect a minister to look like: male, cis, privileged. Compare this with a woman who turns up with sleeves short enough to show off her tattoos. This was in a time when it was not yet fashionable in the mainstream to have tattoos; it was something that 'vulgar', working-class people had. She was a working-class woman who was a candidate to be a deacon. She was evangelical and very charismatic. When we asked her the same question about her call, she told us this story. In a previous life, she had been a sex worker (so you can imagine how well that was going to go down with the bourgeois, middle-class people who are choosing people to represent Jesus and the Church). She said that she was with a client and, suddenly, Jesus broke through her door on a surfboard of fire. As she was telling her story, you could see the eyes proverbially and literally rolling in people's heads: 'What kind of crazy woman is this, who wants to come with her tattooed arms, telling us about Jesus on a surfboard of fire, having been a sex worker?' So we turned her down, because she didn't fit the typology. We then said our prayers at the end of it, convinced that what we had done was in the power of the Holy Spirit. I submit that what we did was in the power of whiteness, of respectability politics, which says who belongs and who doesn't.

There were a fair number of Black and Asian people in the room as well, because whiteness is not just about people's racialization. We know that many communities across the old British Empire have internalized the tropes of whiteness and ended up reproducing it long after white people have gone; for example, all the laws on homosexuality are from colonial times, but people have ended up policing those laws long after the colonial masters have left, because they've internalized whiteness and they think that is what 'proper' Christianity looks like.

Deconstructing whiteness and mission Christianity is not something for people who write books, like me. It's the way in which we bring an element of authenticity back to this corrupted enterprise that has lost its way for over 1,000 years. There's always been a remnant that has been pushing back against all this. At various points, there have been reform movements – not reformed in the traditional, theological sense in how we understand what is authority, etc. but reformed in the sense that they have reminded us that at the heart of our faith is someone who was persecuted and in his own context – a Palestinian Jew.

It's interesting, isn't it, that we somehow decided that it wasn't Pontius Pilate who was to blame for the death of Jesus, but the Jews? The villains were Jesus' own people. This then led to the dangers of anti-Semitism. When thinking about whiteness, we see once more that this comes out of the way in which Gentile Christians become the people of God and Jewishness was pushed to one side as being the 'other'. We end up with a white, Arian Jesus. Christian supersessionism is what allows the Empire to say, 'It was the Jews who killed Jesus – it's very obvious!', but if you read any of the four Gospels, you see that it was the Romans who killed him. Why don't we want to name the Romans as the villains? Because the minute Britain becomes an imperial power, and ends up appointing its own versions of Pontius Pilate in various parts of the world, there's no longer any great appetite to name the Romans as the villains, because if we do that, what we're really doing is convicting ourselves. Britain held the largest empire the world has ever seen – 44,000 square miles of country controlling 24% of the world on which the sun literally never sets.

Conclusion

Deconstructing whiteness is a must in order to have a form of Christianity that has credibility and authenticity in a world in which we are still wrestling with the residues of Empire and colonialism, of top-down power, of the constriction of bodies, of the categorization under the rubric of 'race', where race is a false consciousness, because race does not exist. There is only one race and that's the human race. And yet, the way in which race has infected the body politic, not only of nations but, most crucially, of the Church and of Christianity, has meant that, rather than being a form of resistance against all the things I just mentioned, the Church has colluded with those things for the most part. The reality now is that we find that some of the fastest growing and most popular versions of church are the ones that are the most adept at reiterating and reinscribing all those elements of whiteness that we need to resist and repel.

Part of the way in which we resist and repel whiteness and colonialism is to always take seriously the voices from the margins. One book which I like to read and re-read is a book of that title by the Sri Lankan scholar R. S. Sugirtharajah. In *Voices from the Margins*, he brings together a wonderful cast of scholars from the global majority and they re-read and re-interpret biblical texts from the perspective of the margins. It's one of the earliest iterations of a post-colonial, anti-imperial mindset that says that if Christianity is going to regain its sense of authenticity, we need to hear the voices from the margins that are talking back to the power of whiteness, talking back to the power of empire, talking back to the constriction of respectability politics that clothes some bodies as more of Christ and others as not worth considering. Until that happens, I think our faith will always be compromised. We will always be on the wrong side of historical argument. We will be more analogous to Pontius Pilate than we are to a Palestinian Jew, whose earliest ministry to people on the margins of Empire was to speak truth to power and not to collude with it.

Part of the good news of Inclusive Church is that, at your

best, I want to believe that the things you're trying to do are the very things I'm speaking of. Recognize that deconstructing whiteness is an incredibly difficult thing to do, because of the way in which it has so infected our way of being. However, it is not impossible.

Further Reading

Cone, J., 1970 (new edition 1990), *A Black Theology of Liberation*, Maryknoll: Orbis Books.
Cone, J., 2011 (new edition 2013), *The Cross and the Lynching Tree*, Maryknoll: Orbis Books.
Jennings, W. J., 2010, *The Christian Imagination*, London: Yale University Press.
Jennings, W. J., 2020, *After Whiteness*, London: SPCK.
Reddie, A. G., 2010, *Is God Colour-blind?*, London: SPCK.
Reddie, A. G., 2019, *Theologizing Brexit*, Abingdon: Routledge.
Reddie, A. G., 2022, *Introducing James H. Cone*, London: SCM Press.

Note

1 This chapter is based on the author's 2022 Inclusive Church Annual Lecture.

6

Still Calling from the Edge

FIONA MACMILLAN[1]

Introduction

Since 2012 Inclusive Church have been working in partnership with St Martin-in-the-Fields to host an annual conference on disability and church. It is uniquely *for* rather than *about* disabled people who gather to resource each other and the Church. This is my take on the conference story, beginning with my story and working through the conferences. However, describing a single event each year would only be half the story because the work has rippled outwards in many unexpected ways. As well as writing about the conferences over the years, I will tell you about some ripples and ideas we think are worth sharing.

2012: Opening the Roof

Disabled people often turn to church in the hope of something better than society: a different set of values, a place to belong. In 2011 I was largely housebound, keeping a toe in the door of church but not really feeling at home. Energy, understanding and physical barriers had made church a hard place for me to access then. After an extensive building project bringing ramps and lifts, I found I could get in but not really join in.

This was a time of austerity, relentless news of cuts in government spending and all the things that made it possible to get out and join in society. In the run-up to the Paralympics – set up to laud disabled people as long as we could do something extraordinary – we also had the beginnings of the Welfare Reform Bill and Bedroom Tax. Newspaper stories of 'benefit scroungers' and the rise in disability hate crime made society a hard place for disabled people.

I turned to the Church looking for help. I thought that the Church would be preaching to society about the inherent value of people and the need to build for all, sharing the gospel story of hope with the poor and marginalized, championing those vulnerable to government cuts. I found nothing. The Church of England had cut its budget for work on disability, using the residual funds to employ a part-time theologian to advise the archbishops. I couldn't see anything there for me. How was the Church a place for disabled people at all?

I remember going to see Clare Herbert, who was the first National Coordinator of Inclusive Church and had newly returned to St Martin's as Lecturer in Inclusive Theology. I asked her what the Church was doing. 'Ah,' she said, 'Inclusive Church is doing something! They've expanded their focus to include disability and mental health. Why not check out their website?'

I went off with high hopes and found the website listing a wide range of work. Each area had a bullet point with a drop-down menu, but when I clicked on disability there was no drop-down menu – it was just a bullet point. I went back to Clare who was slightly stumped, but after a long conversation about the issues, she said, 'Leave it with me.' A month or so later Clare was back with an invitation – 'I've spoken to Bob at Inclusive Church about putting on a day conference on disability. We'll do it if you do it with us.'

I knew nothing about putting on a day conference, but luckily Clare and Bob knew a lot. I knew what my needs were and how it felt to be excluded and I wanted to create a space which met the needs of as many disabled people as possible. I understood how it felt to be always asking for access as though for favours, always having to explain what I need and sometimes why. I wanted a space where access was woven into what we did rather than added on, where barriers were understood and accessibility was a culture not a strap-line. So we worked together, meeting every couple of months for around a year and emailing in between. We didn't know what would happen or who, if anyone, would come.

As Clare, Bob and I worked together, we were occasionally joined by others who took on a piece of the day. Rachel Wilson agreed to tell her story of vocation as a woman with cerebral palsy and a stammer who worked for the DWP. God spoke to Rachel in her kitchen and called her to ordained ministry; she was about to be ordained deacon. We invited John Hull, a blind disability theologian, to talk about disabled people, the Bible, and his experience of God. Jane Young, co-founder of the Spartacus movement and a regular writer in the *Guardian*, agreed to talk about disability and society, how to challenge power, and how to make a difference. We made space in the day for small groups because we thought everyone would have a story to tell, and long coffee breaks for unplanned conversation. We also made a silent space for those who needed a break from sound, to lie down and rest, or to pray.

As we wove the plans together, Bob and Clare would often ask me what to do. I would ask what they did when there was a conference on queer theology or feminism, then take their answer and say, 'Like that, but with more time to get around because we'll be queuing for the lift', or 'with more silence and bigger turning circles'. We called it *Opening the Roof* because we were opening a conversation – not beginning the conversation nor coming up with answers, but simply opening a space and to see what would happen.

I felt the responsibility of being the only disabled person on the planning team – the one who instinctively knew what would work but sometimes struggled to put it into words. We agreed that we'd all look after a speaker and a group, Clare would chair the morning, Bob the afternoon, and I'd look after access. I remember sitting alongside registration 30 minutes before we were due to begin, and looking up to see a long queue for the lift. I rejoiced. There were people in different types of wheelchairs, people with walking frames, people with guide dogs. Suddenly there were 40 or 50 of us. I was surrounded by the people I had worked so hard to imagine; here was my tribe. It was a joyous day – full of life, commitment and energy. I genuinely felt that it was a foretaste of the Kingdom.

The First Ripple

This first ripple began the very next day at St Martin-in-the-Fields. I described the experience like this:

> [T]he following day we joined the Sunday morning service and listened to lessons, sang hymns and heard anthems which all used the language of sickness and sin, blindness as lack of insight and choruses of the leaping lame. It was a rude return to reality.[2]

Developing the Sunday service which takes place the day after the conference has been an integral part of our learning as individuals, groups and the whole St Martin's community have explored ideas of disability and healing. The second year there was a leap forward, with a special liturgy for the Sunday morning service written by our lecturer in inclusive theology, with members of our Disability Advisory Group (DAG) reading lessons and intercessions, and assisting with the distribution of communion. The keynote speaker from the conference was a visiting preacher. It was good to be sharing ideas, and it made for a visible presence, but we weren't yet using all our gifts and gathered wisdom.

The next year our vicar, Sam Wells, invited members of the DAG to write parts of the service. We chose readings and set up a liturgy-writing workshop for an hour one Sunday. About a dozen people worked in twos and threes to write a confession, intercessions, invitation and thanksgiving. The result was a service where anyone could lead, read or preach, because disabled people's ideas were woven into the fabric of the liturgy itself.

Sometimes the service brings an opportunity for usually-not-very-visible people to become more visible; participation that might not work on a regular basis can become symbolic as we model the gathered company of saints. One year, a member with Alzheimer's was invited to assist with the distribution of communion. Her vociferous life-long campaigning for women's equality, including women's ordination, had sometimes been coloured by deep disappointment and anger. Here, at the heart of the service, assisted by a faithful friend, she held the ciborium and gazed at each person approaching with a luminous and loving intensity – her weakness transformed into intense presence.

2013: Places of Belonging

In 2013, we focused on mental health precisely because it is usually left out of conversations about disability. John Swinton spoke about stigma and the importance of belonging to an audience where a majority had painful lived experience. Mims Hodson, who was diagnosed with bipolar disorder in 1996, told us:

> One of the most hurtful things that can happen when I am manic is that people walk away because they don't know what to say or do. I believe that one of the biggest causes of exclusion is fear. People are scared they will make things worse. It is OK to say you don't know what to say or do. We are all individuals and have different needs, so just ask how you can help.[3]

Mims became a long-term member of our conference planning team and had some of our best ideas.

2014: Transforming Our Vision

John Hull was hugely encouraging of the conference and agreed to come back as a keynote speaker. Together, we considered vision as sight, insight and hope, and explored the importance of language in naming, understanding and transforming our experience. John was brilliant: in every part of the day, you could have heard a pin drop. He delighted in being among disabled people, marvelling at how we 'just got it'. In his talk, now published, he said:

> Disabled people have a distinct ministry in the church. Disabled people are not so much pastoral problem as a prophetic potential. We need to ask not how the church can care for disabled people but to ask what is the prophetic message of the church in our culture and how disabled people can make a unique contribution to that renewal.[4]

He also said:

> [I]n order for the church to be the church, people with disabilities should accept the church and try to change it from within. There is not so much a question of including disabled people in the church; it is rather a matter of the normal church learning how to welcome those who appear to be different, and in that welcome which embraces difference to rediscover the prophetic calling.[5]

The Second Ripple

Inclusive Church used the conference pattern of centring on lived experience, storytellers and theology for a series of resource books. The first two books, *Disability* and *Mental Health*, included the keynote speakers and conference storytellers from the first three years. The other four books were *Ethnicity*, *Poverty*, *Sexuality* and *Gender*.

2015: Living on the Edge

This was our fourth conference, and we were only just beginning. We explored living where we are without waiting to be included, and invited disabled people from across the country to share how they had used the painful experience of exclusion. We heard from practitioners, campaigners, writers, researchers and advocates, from church building-based and online communities. We all recognized that we were part of something bigger.

To illustrate *Living on the Edge* we used a picture of a path at the edge of a forest. We always put a lot of thought into the images we use. They never have people in them, because someone will always be missed out, but instead seek to resonate with the theme and encourage wondering. Researching the image, I grew to understand:

> The edge of a forest is a very particular habitat, a precise place rather than merely not centre or not outside. Things that would struggle in the centre, would fail to thrive through lack of space or light, would flourish on the edge. And things that would struggle in open ground find shelter and shade on the edge. We too are in a particular habitat. To be on the edge of church or society is not just to be looking inward at where we are not, but to be looking outward at what is beyond and looking around to see who else is there with us. There is a freedom on the edge, a space to grow in different ways, to find shelter and shade, space and light, to learn a different kind of flourishing.[6]

2016: Prophets and Seers

The late John Hull had challenged us to consider whether disabled people have a distinct prophetic ministry to the Church. Our first filmed speaker was Donald Eadie, a Methodist minister living with a disabling spinal condition who had been advocating for disabled people in churches since the 1990s. He told us:

We are learning that theology must not be left to the fit and strong. Theology must also be wrestled for through pain and disability; these are the raw materials of our encounters with a mysterious, silent, hidden and powerless God. It is our experience that the church finds it difficult to receive the gifts of God through those who live with impairments. We are an uncomfortable presence.[7]

Donald also joined us on zoom in 2020, bringing stories of some of the unexpected companions he had encountered on his journey over more than 20 years.

On the Sunday afternoon, we held our first film screening. We screened the film *Notes on Blindness*,[8] based on John Hull's audio diaries as he lost his sight. The film was followed by a discussion with Marilyn Hull and two of the film-makers, Peter Middleton and Jo Jo Ellison. We opened the screening to anyone who was interested – not just the church, but the wider world too! The weekend felt like a fitting tribute to our friend John Hull.

The Third Ripple

To mark five years of conferences, we published a booklet of snippets from speakers and responses from delegates. *Calling from the Edge* was published in 2017. To mark its publication, we held launch events at the Church of England's General Synod and at our conference.

2017: Just as I Am

At the 2017 conference, we considered, 'What does it mean to be disabled and what does that tell us about God? Do our stories tell us something of God's story? Are we living theology?' Two memories in particular stand out for me. The first was the wonderful image of a thumbprint, an inspired idea from Emily

Richardson, a gifted communicator who had just joined the planning team and was running our social media. We chose a thumbprint that looked like a swirling cosmos, bringing together the biggest part of creation with the details at our fingertips.

My second memory is of a delegate I met when I was really tired and only too aware of all that hadn't worked. She told me to keep going because the conference had changed her life, then wrote on her feedback form:

> I came last year to learn tips to take to my church back home and instead found I had been given back to myself. I went home with more confidence to be able to say, 'This is who I am, this is what you can do.' I came back to be restored again and resourced for another year.

2018: Something Worth Sharing

This was a conference that became another booklet, *our fourth ripple*. In the introduction to the booklet, I wrote about the reason:

> It's easy to take what we know for granted. We forget that our 'normal' may have been honed by particular experience, or be the fruit of knowledge developed over many years. To realize that what we have is worth sharing.

Over the last seven years, our conferences have promised 'disabled people gather to resource each other and the church'. And every year at least one person has gone home disappointed. 'You didn't give me any resources,' they say on the feedback form. 'Where are the handouts?'

But there are serious concerns behind their complaint. As others have told us: 'This once a year is wonderful but where I live it's really hard,' 'I want to be part of church but I can't do it the usual way so I can't do it at all,' 'I'm told I'm being demanding – I want to challenge this but don't know where to start,' 'How on earth do we change the church?'

'Looking around the table at a conference planning meeting, we realized that we were taking our own normal for granted. We've been resourced by each other and by the delegates and speakers who have joined us. It is our duty and our joy to share what we know – about access and language, communication and structure, about getting in and joining in. We hope it may enable others to unlock gates and open gifts – because we all have something worth sharing.'[9]

2019: Thinking Differently About God: Neurodiversity, Faith and Church

Neurodiversity is the idea that there are natural variations in the way people think, sense and understand the world. These differences include autism, ADHD, dyslexia, dyspraxia and Tourette's. The topic was something of a leap of faith, as these are often regarded negatively in society and the Church, but we had autistic and other neurodivergent planning team members, so in a sense it was long overdue. In the event, it was also over-subscribed, with more than a hundred delegates and a long waiting list.

We explored our understanding of God and heard stories of discovery, discrimination and discernment. There were a host of wonderful workshops, including identity, imagery and contemplation; Ignatian spirituality; an autistic hermeneutic; neurodiversity and an enhanced social justice imperative; and thinking differently about words. As was our custom, we ended with an informal Eucharist and anointing – not for healing, but to go out and witness in the world.

Rachel Noël is an autistic, ADHD and bipolar priest who joined us for the first time, as a storyteller. Afterwards she wrote to me:

Blown away at the sense of belonging and welcome in the room, of spending the day with so many others that I have ND traits in common with, of shared language and understanding.

A place where all were honoured, where it was safe to be me, each of us children of God ... I know every church says that they are welcoming and that all are welcome. I experienced a radical depth to that welcome today that I've never experienced before. (I feel embarrassed to write this, I'm a vicar, so one would hope that I, at least, would feel welcome in church!)

2020: Telling Encounters

In February 2020, the planning team were all concerned about the new virus Covid-19 – a majority had significant health concerns, so we decided to hold meetings on zoom. Coincidentally, our first meeting was the day after lockdown began in March 2020. Throughout the next six months, we worked to encourage one another and to translate the conference practice to an online forum – accessibility, participation and the building of a community from the day conference. Being online created new barriers for some, but also opened the conference for others who had been unable to participate due to health or geography: new people joined us from bed and from around the world. We shared stories of encountering God in unexpected places and the experience of being disabled people in a global pandemic. In reflecting on this I wrote:

> It is precisely this practice of vulnerability that could enrich society and particularly the Church. Many disabled people have long experience of being unable to access buildings and of building online communities; of reluctantly finding new ways of doing things because the old ways are no longer possible; of suddenly being confined to a space by limited capacity, pain or resources – and of learning to stay still and go deeper. These paradoxical gifts are being overlooked as society and church now colonise the spaces where disabled people dwell, and longed-for adjustments in work and worship are miraculously possible.[10]

Key Ideas

I'd like to share some ideas from our practice and learning which I hope will ripple outwards too:

1. *Disabled people gather to resource each other and the Church.* Disabled people are often isolated by experience or geography – we are likely to be the only voice hearer, wheelchair user, Deaf or autistic person within the local church and community. We face barriers which are invisible to the people around us. Otherness is exhausting; we find our strength by finding each other.
2. *This is disabled-led work.* St Martin-in-the-Fields and Inclusive Church are perfect partners, faithfully resourcing the conference with funds, but more importantly with in-kind resources of colleagues and place, on-site at St Martin's and online with HeartEdge. It is not organizations putting something on about or even for disabled people, but rather working *with* us, holding a space for disabled people to work together, encouraging and affirming us. This is what makes the conference possible.
3. *We prioritize the voices and experience of disabled people.* Much of the time, the voices heard on disability – particularly in the Church – are non-disabled people speaking from research, observation or living alongside loved ones. That is good and important work, but somehow it has become the dominating voice. Observational insight is valuable, but if it is the only perspective heard, it can do damage. There is a power that comes with being heard; this can only happen if disabled people have the resources and opportunities to speak.
4. *We are open to new people.* I see my role as a juggler and juggling as an act of faith. It involves learning to reach out to the edge without looking, trusting that your hand will be filled, catching what comes, holding it without grasping, bringing it into the centre and letting it go. Each year, we invite new storytellers, contributors and staff, and are joined

by new delegates. We are refreshed and renewed by reaching out, drawing from the edge to the centre and letting go.

5 *We are open to new ideas.* For example, in our second year, we added feedback forms, and in our third year, we used them to ask more interesting questions, such as 'What do you want to say to the Church about your experience?' We printed responses and put them on a stall at the Church of England's General Synod, right between the meeting chamber and the coffee room. We literally took people's calls to the Church from the edge to the centre!

When we moved online during the pandemic, we recreated our usual marketplace in a Facebook group, and expanded creative participation through two pre-conference zoom workshops, preparing art and music. We introduced an online chaplaincy as a space to be heard, to share silence or to pray, offering a team of chaplains with a range of disability and faith experience. The day after the conference we hosted a post-conference coffee hangout on zoom to share experience and reflections. We have kept the Facebook group open and continue to hold a monthly coffee gathering to share experience and explore faith. These connections were a lifeline in the isolation of the pandemic; they have become an oasis and a faith community.

Conclusion

I signed up to put on a day conference in 2012, yet here we are more than ten years later. The work is not finished – perhaps it never will be – but something has begun. There is a growing movement of disabled Christians, as people seemingly working in isolation are beginning to find one another, not just in this country but around the world. We share common ideas: theology arising from lived experience; disability as a social justice issue for the Church; the need to move beyond access and inclusion to belonging, full participation and leadership.

Change doesn't always mean doing big things; it can come by

calling from the edge with courage, clarity and persistence. This conference story began with one unhappy person asking questions of the right person at the right time, and has continued thanks to many disabled planners, contributors and delegates – and, of course, our amazing partners. Ten years later, disabled people are still calling from the edge: our call is a lament, a cry for justice and perhaps a mark of prophetic ministry.

Further Reading

www.inclusive-church.org/topics/disability (accessed 13.5.23).

Notes

1 This chapter is based on the author's keynote talk to the 2021 conference.
2 Fiona MacMillan, 'St Luke's Day', in *Liturgy on the Edge*, ed. Sam Wells, Norwich: Canterbury Press, 2018, p. 113.
3 Mims Hodson, 'Miriam's Story', in *Mental Health: The Inclusive Church Resource*, London: Darton, Longman and Todd, 2015.
4 John Hull, 'Theology', in *Disability: The Inclusive Church Resource*, London: Darton, Longman and Todd, 2014, p. 97.
5 Hull, 'Theology', pp. 99–100.
6 Fiona MacMillan and Sam Wells, 'Calling from the Edge', *Plough Quarterly*, 30, 2022, pp. 46–51, at p. 48.
7 Donald Eadie, in *Calling from the Edge*, Inclusive Church/St Martin-in-the-Fields resource booklet, 2017, p. 23; see also https://www.inclusive-church.org/wp-content/uploads/2020/05/Calling-from-the-Edge-printers.pdf (accessed 27.1.23).
8 *Notes on Blindness* (film), 2016, https://www.imdb.com/title/tt5117222/ (accessed 13.5.23).
9 Fiona MacMillan, in *Something Worth Sharing*, Inclusive Church/St Martin-in-the-Fields resource booklet, https://www.inclusive-church.org/wp-content/uploads/2020/05/Something-Worth-Sharing-WEB.pdf (accessed 27.1.23).
10 Fiona MacMillan, in Sam Wells, *Finding Abundance in Scarcity*, Norwich: Canterbury Press, 2021, pp. 152–62, at pp. 153–4.

7

What Might a Trans-Affirming Church Look Like?

JACK WOODRUFF

A Trans-Affirming Church

Outside a flag is flying: six horizontal stripes of rainbow, chevrons of black, brown, blue, pink, white around a yellow triangle with a purple circle within it. Inside the door, two people stand and welcome me in. They introduce themselves, name and pronouns, and I see they're wearing badges too. They ask me for mine. As I walk further into the church, there is a table with leaflets on it. It turns out this church building is used by a variety of groups – Christian and not. The local LGBTQ+ support group meets here; once a month there is a service for LGBTQ+ people and allies; and next week they are having a clothes swap. The service starts, and after a while I realize only gender-neutral language is being used about God. In the prayers, we pray for people who suffer hate for being themselves, and we pray for a system that's fair, and for those in power to take action. It feels genuine. A familiar tune begins to play, and I'm surprised because it's full of patriarchal language, but I look at the order of service, and we sing revised words. At communion, the person celebrating announces, 'All are welcome at this table, regardless of *disability, economic power, ethnicity, gender, gender identity, learning disability, mental health, neurodiversity, or sexuality*', quoting directly from the Inclusive Church vision statement. This might be obvious to some here, but hearing it makes me feel welcome.

After the service, I wander through to the hall for tea and coffee. On a noticeboard is the list of staff and volunteers, with names, pronouns and roles. The church calendar shows an upcoming service to mark Transgender Day of Remembrance. There is a picture of a group standing in the city centre under the banner 'Christians at Pride'. I walk past a door with a sign 'Toilets: All Genders Welcome'. Inside the hall, in one corner, is the church library. They have a wide range of books on sexuality, trans theology, Black liberation theology and disability theology. I walk outside and look around, flag still flying in the breeze, and think: 'This church. They are doing it right.'

To be honest, I have never been to this church, but out there I am sure there is one like it, and I am hoping that over time more and more churches will be like this. This church is my vision for a Church that is not only *inclusive* for trans people, but one that upholds us, affirms us and celebrates us. But how do these things contribute to that vision?

Why Are Pronouns Important?

For two years I lived in the resident community at Iona Abbey working on behalf of the Iona Community. Each week, we met as a whole team, staff and volunteers, and one week a new volunteer introduced himself with his name and pronouns. For example, 'Hello, I am Jack and I use he/him pronouns.' Afterwards, in conversation with others, it became apparent that a lot of people had not encountered the idea of using pronouns to introduce themselves. A large proportion of the team were cisgender,[1] and had never thought about their pronouns before. Most had walked through life without having their gender questioned, or questioning it themselves.

The pronouns we use to talk about each other are important, they are how we relate to the world, and they help identify who we are, just as our name is part of our identity. Pronouns are something we generally assume about each other. When we meet someone, we make a judgement as to what pronoun to use, often based on their body, face, hair, clothes, voice and name. Our brains make these assessments based on gender norms, and what we are taught is 'male' and 'female'. However, not everyone fits into these norms, whether cisgender or transgender. Therefore, it is important to normalize the sharing of our pronouns, because in doing that we are ensuring that everyone is referred to with the correct pronouns, and we are challenging the idea that we should conform to gender norms.

In response to this, I have often heard (cisgender) people say that they don't care what pronouns people use about them, because they aren't there when this happens. But I think they would be surprised by how quickly it would bother them if everyone around them began using the incorrect pronouns about them – both in group conversations, and in their absence. Perhaps it wouldn't be dissimilar to the feeling many feel when their name is repeatedly mispronounced.

Introducing ourselves with pronouns doesn't just challenge gender norms; it also allows some people's gender identity to become more visible. This is particularly true for most, if not all, non-binary people. Non-binary people tend to use they/them pronouns or a mixture of pronouns. There are many non-binary people who, upon meeting them, you might classify as being 'male' or 'female' but allowing them the chance to tell you they use they/them pronouns, you are allowing them to be respected, and referred to in a way that reflects who they are.

It is important to note that for some transgender people it might be hard for them to share their pronouns. This could be because they are not out yet, or they haven't yet discerned what their pronouns are. Some older trans people are also unused to the sharing of pronouns or the idea of people being non-binary. No community is monochrome, including the trans community! Sharing one's pronouns should be optional, but still encouraged. For example, you could say 'You are invited to introduce yourselves with your name, and if you are comfortable doing so, your pronouns.'

After educating my colleagues at the Abbey as to why introducing ourselves with pronouns is important, even if initially it seems like a small, perhaps pedantic exercise, many have now reconciled their hesitations and embrace the practice. Now, every week when we welcome new guests to the Abbey, we invite them to introduce themselves with their names and pronouns. It often surprises me how willing people are to do this. And although I will never know, perhaps there has been a guest come and stay who has felt more comfortable and safer in the Abbey because we have started the week showing that we are taking steps to be more inclusive.

When it comes to pronouns, another increasingly common practice is including pronouns in email signatures. This can be extended to the inclusion of pronouns on noticeboards where members of staff, or committees, are listed. You may remember the fictional church from the story at the beginning with their names, pronouns and roles on the noticeboard.

Hosting Groups

A lot of church buildings have spaces where small groups can meet – either a church hall, meeting rooms, or the main church with flexible seating. Hosting LGBTQ+ groups is a great way to build connections with the local LGBTQ+ community. A lot of these groups are often working with a small budget, so offering them a discounted rate or the building space for free could be extremely valuable to them. By doing this, you are using your church's assets to uplift groups who typically don't have a permanent base. I am sure there are other groups beyond LGBTQ+ ones that could also benefit. Giving meeting space for free might not be your normal church policy, but it would be an act of radical hospitality, which is something that Jesus certainly didn't shy away from.

When churches talk about the inclusion of different minorities, the first thought is usually around how to diversify church membership. However, membership isn't the only thing that churches can offer. Beyond meeting spaces, what else can your church offer? Perhaps a church fundraiser for a charity that helps those you want to reach out to? Perhaps, you could advertise volunteering opportunities with these charities? Could you contact the local groups and charities, and ask them what they might need from you? Is there someone in your congregation who has a certain skillset that they are looking for? By building these links, you are integrating your church further with the local community, and showing people that the church is active beyond Sunday worship. Along the way you might end up with a few new members, even if that is not your primary motivation.

Gender Neutral Spaces

Using gender neutral language to refer to God doesn't only benefit transgender people. Traditionally, God is referred to using he/him pronouns, which confines God to a male identity. However, God goes beyond our human boundaries, and encompasses all of humanity. In the Genesis creation myth, humankind is created in the image of God (Genesis 1.26). We begin to glimpse a more expansive image of God by bringing all of humanity into that image. God is neither male nor female, God encompasses all genders, whilst at the same time being beyond gender. By referring to God using gender neutral language, our language is beginning to reflect the expansiveness of God. It is important that all people are able to relate to God in a way that works for them. For some, referring to God as 'mother' or using she/her pronouns can be empowering. Likewise, the same goes for referring to God with he/him pronouns or they/them pronouns. The main thing is that we don't exclusively use male language around God, because this doesn't work for everyone.

For some trans people, there is a lot of anxiety around using public toilets. Traditionally, these are gendered spaces, so for some trans people there can be an additional pressure to 'pass', which means to be perceived by others as the gender they're presenting as. This pressure and anxiety can be reduced with gender neutral toilets. This means there is no expectation as to who should and shouldn't be in this space.

Transgender Day of Remembrance

Each year, on 20 November, communities across the globe mark Transgender Day of Remembrance. This tradition began in 1999 by transgender advocate Gwendolyn Ann Smith as a vigil to honour the memory of Rita Hester, a transgender woman who was killed in 1998. As Smith says herself,

> Transgender Day of Remembrance seeks to highlight the losses we face due to anti-transgender bigotry and violence. I am no stranger to the need to fight for our rights, and the right to simply exist is first and foremost. With so many seeking to erase transgender people – sometimes in the most brutal ways possible – it is vitally important that those we lose are remembered, and that we continue to fight for justice.[2]

Traditionally, the names of all transgender people who have been murdered in the past year are read out.[3] So often we reduce people to numbers: the number of people fleeing war, the number of people unemployed, the number of people murdered. By reading the names, we go beyond the numbers and try to see the individual lives that have been lost. However, the names we do have are only a snapshot of the bigger picture. It is near impossible to estimate the number of unreported cases, due to data not being systematically collected in all countries, misgendering and denial of a person's trans identity after they die, and then there are those who commit suicide because the transphobia surrounding them becomes too much.

Something that churches often excel at is creating a space where vigils can be held, a place beyond the chaos of daily lives. Churches can provide a space where trans (and cis) people of all faiths can gather to mark TDOR and mourn those lost. Each year, a growing number of liturgies are available. For example, *Stones and Bread, Mourning and Joy* by Alex Clare-Young includes an act of remembrance, intercessions and other resources specifically for TDOR. Another date you can mark in your calendar is Transgender Day of Visibility, held on 31 March.

Being Visible

The flag I described at the beginning of this chapter is a new adaptation to Daniel Quasar's Pride Progress flag. The 6 rainbow stripes echo the early pride flags, and represent sexual orientation – the LGBQ(+) in LGBTQ+, i.e. lesbian, gay, bisexual, queer people etc. The black and brown chevrons represent LGBTQ+ people of colour, who are often more vulnerable to discrimination due to systemic and overt forms of racism, and whose voices often go unheard in LGBTQ+ discourse. The pink, blue and white chevrons represent transgender and non-binary people. The purple circle on the yellow background is a new adaptation which represents intersex people. The new design is by Valentino Vecchietti of Intersex Equality Rights UK.[4] Showing this flag in a visible place is a very clear signal that you are LGBTQ+ inclusive.

Another way to be visible is to engage with your local pride events. This could be through walking in the pride parade, having a stall if possible, or hosting events in your church building. There might be churches nearby who are already involved with pride, who you could team up with. A lot of churches walk under the 'Christians at Pride' banner.[5]

Why Include Trans People?

Why is it so important that we include transgender people in our churches? First, because we are called by God to do so. The answer is simple, but by no means easy to put into action. We are called by God, through the words attributed to Jesus, 'You shall love your neighbour as yourself' (Matthew 22.39). Our neighbours are the people we live alongside, the people we encounter in the world around us, and that is everyone. To me, Jesus is all about radical inclusion. He ate with the social outcasts of the day, and he spoke to all people, not just the ones society approved of at the time. Christian or not, that is what our mission here is. To be Christ-like is to practise radical inclusion. By standing up for trans rights and/or living as our true transgender selves, we are advocates for radical inclusion.

Radical inclusion is also a commitment to justice, and a commitment to liberation. Society as a whole is still a hostile place for trans people. Transphobic attacks and behaviours are on the rise in the UK with 2,630 hate crimes against transgender people reported in 2020–21. This statistic becomes even more shocking when the National LGBT Survey reported that 88% of transgender people did not report hate crimes they experienced.[6] Shon Faye presents an analysis of the current situation for trans people, and the pressing need for trans liberation in her book *The Transgender Issue*. I strongly recommend reading this book as a first step. By understanding the issues trans people face, you might find different ways your church can advocate for trans liberation.

The ways listed above might read as superficial compared to calls for liberation and justice. However, it is important to start somewhere. Historically, as an institution the Church has been hostile to LGBTQ+ people. Through personal experience, I have found that a lot of people still assume this about churches. In some cases, this assumption holds true, which is why it is important for churches that are inclusive to be as visible as possible about this. If the default assumption is that a church will be transphobic, then it is the responsibility of churches where this is not the case to be openly trans-affirming. Further practical tips for this can be found in Christina Beardsley and Chris Dowd's book *Trans Affirming Churches: How to Celebrate Gender-Variant People and Their Loved Ones* (2020). Once your church becomes visibly inclusive to trans people, the next important step would be to begin looking at ways you can push for trans liberation.

Notes

1 Cisgender is the opposite of transgender, i.e., someone whose gender matches what they were assigned at birth.

2   https://www.glaad.org/tdor (accessed 18.11.22).
3   The list is published annually on https://transrespect.org/en/.
4   https://www.consortium.lgbt/intersex-inclusive-flag/ (accessed 5.12.22).
5   https://www.christiansatpride.com/ (accessed 30.12.22).
6   https://www.stophateuk.org/about-hate-crime/transgender-hate/ (accessed 5.12.22).

8

Carnival and Chaos!

JUNE BOYCE-TILLMAN[1]

The Pointless Child

Once upon a time, there was a land called the Pointed Land. It was so called because everything had a point. All the buildings were pointed. They pointed with sharp points to the sky, but some of them also had points sticking out of them, which meant that people bumped into them and were hurt by them. All the people who lived in the land had points on the top of their heads.

Everything was pointed in the Pointed Land. Even vegetables that were naturally round were grown so they could be pointed, and the ones that weren't pointed were rejected. Into that land, a lovely couple called Jim and Alice were looking forward to the birth of their first child. They had longed for a child for so long, and when the birth came, they were excited – so excited. As the head emerged ... there was no point. Their lovely baby girl had no point on the top of her head. What were they to do?

Well, the doctors were quite clear about what they were to do. She would be pointless. She would never have a life. There'd be no place for her. People would laugh at her. People would bully her. On they went about what a dreadful life their child would have. She would have to be put away. They had special places for children like her, where they kept them away from the pointful people. These were the asylums for the pointless. But Jim and Alice had longed for this child. She was their child, and they said, 'No. We're going to keep her. We're going to make beautiful hats which will disguise the fact that she has no point. They will be lovely, and people will admire them.' The doctors were sceptical, but Alice and Jim won out, and they made pointed hats in beautiful colours for their daughter, whom they called Ublia.

Ublia grew up in the land of points, the Pointed Land. She grew up among a group of women with her hat firmly in place, so nobody could see that she was pointless. The national game of the Pointed Land was called 'triangle toss'. This involved a very pointed triangle which people had to catch on the point on their head. The game was not open for women to play, but it brought a lot of fame and a lot of fortune to the male champions. The most famous player was Maximus Maximus, the son of the ruler of the land.

Maximus was the many-times champion, but the women were sad at not being able to play the game and so they were forming a women's group of triangle toss players. Ublia was in that group, as many of them were her friends. It took a long time before she revealed to them that she had no point, but eventually she did. Fortunately for her, she had a very faithful dog called Fido, and the girls and women of the society got together and thought that they could make it possible for Ublia to play the triangle toss if Fido sat on her head and the triangles were caught by Fido. The combination of Fido and Ublia were so skilled that they challenged Maximus to a contest. Well, Maximus thought this was a stupid contest. Of course, he'd meet the stupid woman who really didn't have any point anyway, so off they went, but the cooperation between Ublia and Fido defeated Maximus.

This did not please Maximus' father and the result of it was that he banished Ublia and Fido to the Pointless Forest. In the forest, they discovered that the trees there were not all pointed. Some of them were, but some of them were round and had round leaves. They dropped their leaves, and the leaves fertilized the earth underneath the trees. When they looked at the earth, they saw round creatures like worms and snakes in the earth burrowing through the earth. They realized that in general the creatures of the earth were round, and that the earth needed round creatures in order to exist. They met a man who did have lots of points because he was made of rocks, but he was looking for his heart which he'd lost somewhere. Then, out of the woodland, came three fat women and they danced, and they danced, and they danced, and Fido and Ublia had a wonderful time joining in the dance.

They also met a tree who said that if all the trees were the same shape, the diversity of the forest would indeed be pointless. The tree showed them that all the creatures they'd met had a point. They all had a place. After several nights in the forest, Fido and Ublia awoke one morning with a large hand in front of them, pointing a finger to show them the direction they should now take, so they followed the hand as it led back to the Pointed Land.

Ublia was no longer wearing her hat, and she came back telling of her journey through the Pointless Forest. She told the people of the Pointed Land that it was untrue that anybody or anything was pointless, and that everything had a point and a meaning. She returned at a good time, because by then the people of the Pointed Land had already staged a rebellion against their dreadful ruler and his son, and they hailed Ublia as a heroine and believed her story. As they did this, all the pointed things started to grow into rounder shapes and to grow roots deeper into the earth so that they were no longer precariously rooted only to the sky, and the three fat women from the forest appeared and danced their liberating dance which everybody then joined in joyously.

Perfection

The story above is based on one by a singer called Nilsson, which has been readapted for this context. It contains many of the elements I'll be exploring in this chapter. How did we get to the point where many people were excluded from the Church, when Jesus says that the Kingdom of Heaven is within not one group of people but within everyone? Over and over again, those are his words. The Kingdom of Heaven is embodied in the bodies of everyone, diverse as they are, and early Christianity, like its roots in Judaism, had no images – no human images – of Jesus, but just patterns and metaphors. These were similar to the patterns that we see in Jewish and Islamic cultures today.

When Christianity met with Greek culture and wanted to convert the Greeks and the Romans, we start to see images of human Jesus in the model of Apollo, the young, athletic male god, with his father Zeus, sporting a beard. Once this happened, Christianity sold out to Greek mythological thinking and lost the idea that the Kingdom of Heaven is within many of you. You will no doubt know the platonic view of reality – the cave – in which we're looking out into a landscape where there's a perfect form of everything. Many of you will know that there's a perfect form of table to which all tables aspire. I don't know whether tables are upset about not being the right table, but certainly it's done human beings no good – this idea that there is a perfect form of the human being. It is perhaps epitomized in many of the renaissance sculptures like David, the young, athletic, male, white person etc. It has served the Church and the world very badly.

There is also the similar idea, which was put forward in the Pythagorean system of geometry, that there is a perfect order at the heart of the universe that we should aspire to. This is particularly an area that I know a lot about, being a musician. There have been many claims made that European music is very close to this order. Make what you will of that! In fact, at the time of Pythagoras there were many other mathematicians setting out other forms of order which were not accepted because Pythagoras had the ear of those in power.

All of these notions of perfection have had a disastrous effect on inclusion in the Church. The phrase from the Bible that has been used to support all of this has been 'be perfect as your Father in heaven is perfect' (Matthew 5.48), but the notion that we could know what God regards as perfect is indeed a very dangerous one. God regards all the embodied shapes of human beings as God-given – we all bear the 'imago dei' and God became incarnate as one of us and suffered, was wounded and died. He did not live a 'perfect' life. Therefore, this Greek notion that became part of Christianity has a Greek philosophical root rather than a Christian or Jewish one. This idea of perfection has been used for empire and to control people. It has meant that liturgy is also tightly controlled, so that even musically it has driven imperialism by wiping out indigenous sounds and movements when it encounters them, by replacing them with European instruments and singing styles. It has also meant that more and more people, for reasons of disability, age, ethnicity, sexuality, gender, poverty etc. have been pushed to the margins or out of the conversation altogether.

Chaos and Disruption

How can Christianity regain the radical hospitality that characterized the ministry of Jesus? Radical hospitality is often interpreted as making people welcome, and that is of course important. However, it's not only about making people welcome and getting them to sit down and behave like everyone else in church. It's about asking what gifts these diverse groups of people in various embodied shapes bring and how can those gifts be incarnated in our worship? This may mean that a lot of the order we've prized so highly will be disrupted.

The hymn I like least is 'Thou whose almighty Word Chaos and darkness heard, And took their flight'. I think we need to have more chaos and more carnival in our worship, because that means that the diverse ways of knowing and being and the shapes of people will be acknowledged and celebrated. Let me give you some examples of what this might look like. In one of the churches in which I worship, we have a very lively four-year-old. She's a scooter rider, and the church is large. Periodically, she will appear suddenly from one side of the church on her scooter, cross in front of the chancel and disappear on the other side. Some people think that she should be under control, that we can't worship God with a scootering child in the House of God. I think it's a wonderful symbol of the Holy Spirit coming – we know not when – exciting us for a little while and then disappearing. How will we include people in the late stages of dementia, people with learning difficulties, or indeed those with Tourette's, who are likely to offer words which may be not part of our liturgy, if we cannot even deal with children being children?

Is the scootering child not an example of everything being brought into worship? The whole of creation is being brought in, including unusual words for some people present. Is that not what worship is about? Another example of bringing the totality of our world into the liturgy in a place where I worship too is Pentecost Sunday, when one of the elders of the church who can no longer walk very well but, when we have the reading of the Gospel in various languages that day, has the microphone brought to her so that she can read in Latin. The Revd Rachel Noel, who is part of the planning committee for the Inclusive Church and St Martin-in-the-Fields Conference on Disability and Church, has introduced knitting and crocheting for people in her church who find it difficult to concentrate. On Prison Sunday, I have had people remark to me that we have a lot of talking from prison chaplains, but very seldom do we have ex-offenders talking about their experiences of prison. Why are they unwilling to share their stories – are their stories not part of the incarnation story too? Have we made them feel uncomfortable about sharing in church settings? Are their stories too 'chaotic'?

What movements are permitted in our overly ordered worship? I was in Rome for a large mass, and I saw all the cardinals and the priests moving their hands in various well-adjusted ways. Then a concert was moved into the chapel, which involved young women singing and dancing. People said that they could not dance in that way in front of the altar. Why was one form of movement acceptable and another form of movement involving young women's bodies not acceptable? Who says that one movement is acceptable and another movement is not acceptable? Other traditions beyond the Catholic and Protestant traditions – for example, the Orthodox traditions – have people moving around freely for part of the service kissing icons and lighting candles and so on, but the Protestant traditions have been particularly controlling of what takes place within the service and the church.

I instituted a service – or, rather, more of a celebration – in Winchester Cathedral, called Space for Peace. People of all the great faiths and none came, and in the middle section they sang all around the cathedral choosing when they would sing, and the cathedral would mix the Rabbi chanting lamentations with the Imam chanting the call to prayer and the children singing. I thought to myself, what a wonderful world. Then they came together and sang together, and people wandered around praying, listening, sitting, contemplating, treating the event as they wanted to treat it. It was true freedom. Some people likened it to a celestial sweet shop. Carnival came into the church. How much carnival can we allow into the church, how much diversity can we accommodate, and how do we do it? That's the question I want to ask in this chapter.

I've learned a lot from Mary Magdalene, who I think represents another tradition which we've lost, or which was dismissed relatively early in the history of the Church, when (according to Provençale tradition) she was put in a boat without a paddle and ended up in the Camargue. In the Gospel of Mary Magdalene, we read this:

> After saying this, the Blessed One greeted them all saying,
> Peace be with you
> May my Peace be fulfilled within you.
> Be vigilant and
> Allow no one to mislead you
> By saying 'Here it is' or 'There it is'
> For it is within you that
> The Son of Man dwells.[2]

Over and over again, in the visionary experiences of Mary Magdalene, we see Jesus the teacher appearing and saying, 'it is within you'. It is not within that perfect person or this perfect person, but within you. Your body has that within you. And over and over again, in the area of inclusion, we've forgotten that message of Jesus.

When you are scanning the face of the other, what do you see, what do you see? Do you see faith underneath the worn wrinkles? Do you see hope among blotches and scars? Do you see joy in the flick of an eyebrow? Do you see freedom behind iron bars? When you are scanning the face of the other, what do you see, what do you see? Do you see Christ in the fierceness of frowning? Do you see God in the brow's forward lines? Is there the Spirit beneath the exhaustion, freeing the soul from the living that binds? When you are scanning the face of the other, what do you see, what do you see? Jesus saw under the masks of a lifetime, saw through the fearing, the yearn of the heart, cut through the knotting of cultures dividing, with a deep incarnation that is wisdom's art. When you are scanning the face of the other, what do you see, what do you see? We would look deeply at faces before us, not be deceived by the differences there. Look with the eyes of the faith of respecting, seeing a world that is holy and fair. When you are scanning the face of the other, what do you see, what do you see?[3]

How far can we disrupt even our cultural perceptions of human bodies? Well, to a certain extent the Covid crisis disrupted our liturgy. Our wonderful priest at All Saints Tooting put together films to represent the liturgy during lockdowns. Mae put together films of people reading in their garden. Folk sent in films from Ghana, Nigeria etc., and congregation members read from their living room, with icons set up behind them. Sometimes people were just sitting at their kitchen tables, meaning that already Covid times have brought a level of intimacy to the congregation that we have never known before. I have seen so much more about the people around me in church than I did when I was simply sitting next to them in church. Ruth Wells wrote a lovely poem in lockdown:

CARNIVAL AND CHAOS!

God snuck home.
No longer bound by the expectations of a
'consecrated' building.
She's concentrated her efforts on breaking out.
Now in the comfort of a well worn dining table she
Shares some bread, with some friends.
And she laughs.
And she weeps. In the sacred space of home.[4]

If our lives have been opened up in that way and we have seen the sacred place of home, how can we carry that on now we're back in church buildings? I want to share a poem that I wrote:

I was alone in the church, the vaults curved around me
And I heard a scratching on the roof
Under the floor, on the door
And at all the windows
And there was a rushing mighty wind
And a figure flew in
I had not seen one like it before
For her flame filled the temple and her skirt flowed with
　serpents
Her hair was filled with honeysuckle and old man's beard
Frogs lipped from her mouth and played around the statues
They found the font and the figure sprayed water from her toes
And the font filled, and the frogs laughed and spewed out
　tadpoles
And some children rushed in and thought it was such fun
I saw that the floor was becoming transparent
I could see the traversing worms, the burrowing beetles, the
　termites and the ants
And then I noticed the roof was filling with birds
They were attached to the strings in her hair
Branches were growing out of the walls
And suddenly a fully grown oak tree leaped out of the floor
No sooner was it born than ivy started to wind itself around
　the trunk

89

And then I saw people were emerging from her belly of every
    shape and every age
They hopped, they jumped, they crawled, they limped, they
    lay on her arms
And started to find places in the corners of the church
And I noticed she was a woman struggling to birth all these
    creatures
For some were minute and some were huge
They contained every rainbow colour
Some were still, some moved,
Some appeared to be made of wood and stone
And the winding ivy and the honeysuckle fronds bound
    them tightly together
Who are you? I said, enveloped in the swirling of the multi
    various creatures
And she replied, I am the wild goddess, thank you for letting
    me in
I have waited so long
She raised her hands, and the vines circled from them,
    dropping grapes
All were trodden and the wheelchairs ploughed over them
The juice flowed into the silver cups which were appearing
    everywhere,
Shaped from buttercups and daffodils
And all drank together
I am joy, she said
And we all laughed, and the sound filled the temple

'Queering' Sacred Spaces

How far can we queer[5] our sacred spaces? How much of the wildness can we let in? Queering the table has become a feature of queer theology in the area of language in liturgy. Some of us have struggled with inclusive language, and the pressure was much greater early in the noughties or indeed in the nineties than it is now. We did have a lot of material, but now we've reverted to the male, somewhat disembodied God, or with a very limited form of body. Some people have been concerned by the pursuit of light and the putting down of darkness in religious language. This has been damaging to people of colour – the notion of dark being evil and white being good has not done much good for the global majority.

I want to look at music, because the problems of exclusion, snobbery and imperialism are rife in that discipline. I mentioned before that the Pythagorean views of knowing the right scale and being in tune with the universe led to the idea of European music being the only 'perfect' music. This is actually just one way of seeing the universe and not necessarily the only way, of course. Bertram Schirr, in his work on queering congregational singing, has talked about how we've got disembodied notions of acoustics which don't bear relation to the bodies of the people who are there.[6] Pythagoras was followed by Clement of Alexandria, with the notion of the ordered bodied of Christ. We should be ordered, because the body of Christ is ordered. That triumphant, disembodied, acoustic body of Christ has been exclusion: the excluding of many people. It's been an area of colonization, disciplining and categorization into race, with particular skin colours, class, a certain control of emotion, gender, pitch, ability to read, literacy, and order of voices making certain bodies expendable.

There is that notion of the perfect sound, epitomized by such places as King's College Cambridge and the Nine Lessons and Carols, which many people love and that's fine, but it is not 'perfect' and nor should it be the only sound considered good or more worthy of being heard in church, or better than any other music from around the world. A Jesuit monk in America produced a wonderful statement: King's College Cambridge has done for music what Barbie has done for women. Indeed, it's presented an impossible image for most people, because it is male, it is white, it is expensive, and so on. Rather than asking what the average church choir with two older women in it can do, why do we always make our choirs aspire to do the David Wilcox descants? Why do we not ask ourselves what any group of people can do liturgically, and do well, rather than aspiring to do something other than that which they can do? We should re-embody liturgy in the bodies of the people who are actually there at the time, with their own variety of gifts.

Bertram Schirr talks about vulnerability. Are we not allowed to share our vulnerability in church? Are older women not allowed to sing in what some people might call a much harsher voice? Can we not allow the late stages of dementia to move through our songs? We all have a mixed vocal range anyway, which changes during our lifetime, so can we not include everyone, rather than having people say, 'I can't sing', when what they really mean is 'I can sing but not in a style that is acceptable in this particular church'? So queering our singing and letting everyone sing when they want to, and letting older women sing in voices that are associated with maleness (as voices get lower with age) is important. It's especially important that we queer how we feel about tone and gender, when we get into the area of our transgender siblings, some of whom may have voices that we may not think match their gender. Let them all sing! Let everyone sing, young and old, all genders, and all abilities.

We had a wonderful young man singing falsetto once in one of our choirs at the university where I worked. He was coming to grips with his own sexuality and had been told by his school that he should sing in the 'proper' male voice, but he challenged everything. He wanted to sing falsetto. When we went to festivals and the choir director would say 'ladies', he put his hand up and said 'I'm here'. A wonderful challenge. All people are welcome, of a variety of ages, disabilities and shapes. You are able to sing even in your most vulnerable voice, the voice that we so often exclude.

Conclusion

What I have said about inclusion is that we have disembodied Christianity in favour of an ideal image. This image is a philosophical image bearing very little relation to our actual bodies, except that it is an image which makes us feel shame and guilt about our own bodies – those same bodies in which God has chosen to frame us. That of course is true of many of the images of God that we have in our churches – the images of a white, male Christ figure, which has disempowered many people. The ceiling of the Sistine chapel, beautiful as it may be in aesthetic terms, reflects a particular view of a particular culture, and it has done the incarnated essence of Christianity – the Kingdom of God within everyone – no good. Indeed, Richard Dawkins may be right that we have for a long time lived with a delusion. It is a guarded illusion. For unless God can be portrayed in a huge variety of images, there is no image that can contain God.

Perhaps we need to revert to the patterns of our Jewish and Muslim brothers and sisters – using only patterns for God instead of images might be better. There is a reason idolatry is so high in the list of the ten commandments – it is exclusive. When you have only limited images of God, people who don't fit those images are excluded from the Kingdom. I first came across a female image of God with a body resembling mine, which is somewhat large, when I went to Malta and saw the goddesses with their heads chopped off (probably by Christians). In my sixties, as I was then, I thought 'I have been in the church all of my life, and I have never seen an image of God that resembles me'. What a tragedy.

I think we have to rethink our images, although in the hymn I'm going to end with I do say that I miss Father God. There's no reason why we shouldn't see God as a Father, but we also need to see God in a wheelchair, to see a Black God, to see a female God, to see God as a toddler, to see God as a person on a deathbed. We need those images, because if we don't have them all, the people in those positions will be excluded not only in the words of our liturgy but in the songs that we sing and the way that we respond to people when they come to church.

To go back to the story at the beginning, are some of the people who come to our churches pointless, or does everyone have a point? We all have a particular gift to offer the liturgy and how we use them all is the challenge. We need to queer the liturgy. We do not need to ask how people can conform – how we can get people in wheelchairs up steps by ramps etc., but instead how we move the altar down, as disability theologian Nancy Eiseland suggests, so that everybody can get there without any steps.

We need to re-think all that we've assumed to be essential – indeed, perfect – to see perfection as variety instead, and to not see unity as equalling uniformity. We need to admit what some people might call the chaos, or the vulnerability, or the brokenness, or simply the diversity of the body of Christ that we as human beings and indeed the other inhuman world represent.

FINDING GOD[7]

1. A child once loved the story
Which angel voices tell –
How once the King of Glory
Came down on earth to dwell.

2. Now, Father God, I miss you –
Your beard, your robes, your crown
But you have served us badly
And let us humans down.

3. So easy to disprove you
And doubt your truthfulness;
For you were just an idol
That kept Your power suppressed.

4. For You are deep within us –
Revealed within our deeds,
Incarnate in our living
And not within our creeds.

5. No image cannot hold you;
And, if to one we hold,
We keep some from your loving
And leave them in the cold.

6. Excluded groups are legion –
Disabled, female, gay –
Old Father of the heavens,
Your picture moves away.

7. Life's processes reveal You –
In prison, death and war,
In people who are different,
In gatherings of the poor.

8. For Godding means encounter,
Gives dignity to all,
Has every shape and no shape –
In temple, tree and wall.

9. So we will go a-godding
And birth You in our world;
In sacrificial loving
We find Your strength unfurled.

Notes

1 This chapter is based on the author's 2020 Inclusive Church Annual Lecture.
2 Gospel of Mary Magdalene p. 7, vv. 13–20. Editor's note: For more on Mary Magdalene and the Gospel of Mary Magdalene, Esther de Boer's *Mary Magdalene: Beyond the Myth* is both scholarly and accessible.
3 This paragraph is based on a hymn written by June herself.
4 Ruth Wells, 'God Snuck Home', https://twitter.com/ruthmw/status/1256317999792832512 (accessed 15.5.23); also quoted at https://thepattas.blogspot.com/2020/05/whom-are-we-serving-at-our-services-we.html (accessed 15.5.23).

5 Editor's note: June is using the term 'queer' here in the sense of 'queer theory', which is an academic discipline linked to but not only about the LGBTQ+ community. It is also about doing everything and anything differently from the 'norm' and about 'the methodology of deconstruction'. See more at https://www.oxfordreference.com/display/10.1093/oi/authority.20110803100358573;jsessionid=1B680EA9C638D56AC75616837C81D612 (accessed 15.5.23) and https://haenfler.sites.grinnell.edu/subcultural-theory-and-theorists/queer-theory/ (accessed 15.5.23).

6 https://www.vr-elibrary.de/doi/10.13109/path.2019.108.3.83 (accessed 15.5.23).

7 In June Boyce-Tillman, 'Rebalancing the Tradition – Wisdom Theology in Hymnody', *International Journal for the Study of the Christian Church*, 21(2), pp. 98–119, doi: 10.1080/1474225X.2021.1997036.

9

The Church of the Future

RUTH WILDE[1]

An Inclusive Gospel

As Dan said in the Introduction to this book, Inclusive Church has been going since 2003. We began working only in the Church of England, but now we are ecumenical. I am the first non-Anglican National Coordinator, straddling (as I do) the Methodist and Quaker traditions. Back in 2003, Inclusive Church was also only really working on sexuality and gender, by which I mean women's equality – transgender inclusion was not yet on the agenda. Now we work across the board on inclusion. As it says in our values statement, we believe in a Church in which 'all people ... grasp how wide and long and high and deep is the love of Jesus Christ'.

If there is one thing I know about the Church of the future, it's that it *must* be inclusive. Firstly, it must be inclusive in order to survive, and there's been some good research into this, including the report I referred to in Chapter 1, 'Leading Together in Growing Methodist Churches'.[2] Arguably even more importantly, though, the Church of the future must also be inclusive in order to build the Kingdom of God. This is, after all, the Church's primary calling.

The Kingdom of God is a phrase Jesus uses in the Gospels, but there is one Gospel in which it isn't mentioned – the Gospel of John. Many scholars believe this is because the author's idea of 'eternal life' is the equivalent concept. The 'Kingdom of God'[3] – or the 'Kingdom of Heaven' – and 'Eternal Life' are ways of talking about a *quality* of life, or the life of God. For the writer of John's Gospel, this is something we can all participate in, starting from now. We are called to become one with God, to be part of God's life, and we do this by becoming more like God, which means imitating Jesus. Jesus' love, as the Inclusive Church statement says, is 'wide and long and high and deep', and that love is demonstrated in the Gospel stories over and over again, especially for those rejected by society, those who are cast aside, for whom life is made more difficult, often because of prejudice and discrimination.

John's Gospel has many examples of Jesus reaching out first and foremost to marginalized people. It is the only Gospel that contains the story of the Samaritan woman at the well, for example. Jesus ignores social norms and the disapproval of the disciples and speaks to a woman one-to-one – not only a woman, but a woman from a religious group which was despised by his own religious group. He has a long and theologically complex conversation with her – longer and in more depth than any other conversation in the Gospel. He breaks down barriers and raises up a woman who has been rejected by her own community, making *her* the one with the power and gift of the knowledge of who he is. She is the one who is chosen and sent to bring *them* – the ones who rejected her – into the Eternal Life of God's Kingdom. She 'saves' them, just as the Church will be only saved by listening to those it has rejected and marginalized, only by becoming radically inclusive, as Jesus was.

It's also only in John's Gospel that we find the story of the wedding at Cana. This is the first 'sign' or miracle in the Gospel and, as such, contains an enormous amount of symbolism. When Jesus turns the water into wine, it is not only so that he can show his power; more importantly, it sets out his intention to include those who have been formerly excluded. It is no coincidence that Jesus takes the purification water, which was meant to ritually exclude some and include others, and turns it into a drink that all can enjoy – a drink of celebration and inclusion (although, nowadays, we might prefer to make the wine non-alcoholic to be even more inclusive of those who struggle with alcohol addiction).

The other Gospels also contain many stories of Jesus' radical inclusion – of Jesus turning the tables on power and privilege. In all four Gospels, we find the story of Jesus literally turning the tables over in the temple. Jesus sees injustice and it makes him angry. In this story, the chief priests who are in charge of the temple sacrifice system control and exclude poor people by making it impossible to participate in worship without spending money that they often do not have. Jesus not only enters the temple, speaks to people in the temple and takes up space; but he *sabotages* the whole system which was put in place to control and hold power over ordinary people.

Jesus' act is almost the exact opposite of what the violent protesters did in the United States government building – the Capitol – in 2021. Whereas those protesters tried to silence the will of ordinary people by stopping democracy, Jesus took drastic action to change things for those who have no power and could not participate in the system. *This* kind of direct action could instead be compared perhaps to the actions of those who pulled down statues or took to the streets in 2020 because no one listened to them about racial inequality and institutional racism – these people were also tired of being silenced and controlled by those in power.

How often have you heard the interpretation I've given above of the cleansing of the temple in church? Far too often, churches sit on the fence or actively prevent change from happening when it comes to the inclusion of Black or poor voices and experiences. Our churches have become too comfortable – we are more interested in criticizing the methods of those who use direct action to make change happen than we are in listening to their frustration and pain. This is what Anthony Reddie calls the 'politics of respectability'. The Church should have no time for respectability politics, just as Jesus had no time for it.

The Church is no longer fulfilling its calling when it stops hearing the cry of those who are harmed and rejected by society. As Mukti Barton explains in the Inclusive Church book on Ethnicity, this is the biblical phenomenon of sighted people who cannot 'see' and non-deaf people being unable to 'hear' (Mark 8.18).[4] Although many deaf and disabled people find this kind of language used in the Bible problematic (it can be harmful to hear disability described negatively all the time, and it feeds into the overarching narrative in society of disability being a negative thing), the point of Jesus' analogy here is to criticize those who wilfully ignore suffering, injustice and exclusion. That is something the Church needs to 'hear' urgently.

Dispelling Shame

It's not only respectability politics which means that Christians fail to act on injustice when we should. Sometimes it's a lack of education, which is why Inclusive Church is primarily an educational charity. Other times it's shame and the fear of failure which prevents us from changing and becoming more inclusive. The survey I mentioned in Chapter 1, by the charity Scope, showed that 67% of people in the UK feel 'uncomfortable' when talking to a disabled person.[5] They fear 'saying the wrong thing', and so prefer to say nothing at all. But we're *all* imperfect and we *all* will make mistakes, no matter how good our intentions are. We can't put our discomfort and shame above the needs of others.

Who suffers most when disabled people are not spoken to and included because of our fear of failure and shame? About a week after I started as the National Coordinator of Inclusive Church, I drove to my choir practice and parked my car right in the way of a wheelchair ramp. Someone from the organizing committee had to come and find me in front of everyone and ask me to move my car. I was mortified. I felt ashamed, not least because I had told some of the choir members about my new job. I learnt some valuable lessons though that day – to be more aware of wheelchair ramps; to think more like a wheelchair user and consider their experience of life more instead of assuming that my experience is universal; and finally, to be humble enough to accept when I've made a mistake, swallow my pride, listen, and change. Justice and solidarity should be our primary motivations as Christians; not comfort and avoidance of shame.

There are times when we need to work on being proud and dispelling a lifetime of shame. For example, when we come out as gay or bi or trans, or our child does, we have to proudly throw off the shackles of societal and church pressure to conform, to be a certain way, to have a certain type of family. This is when pride in ourselves and our children is well placed and necessary. I came out as gay to my parents when I was 20, and first I, and then they, had to go through the process of shaking off the shame of being constantly told that who I am is 'wrong'. This shame can have devastating consequences when unaddressed, and it would be far better if we stopped the negative messaging in society and the Church in the first place. In the Epilogue of this book, you will read of the tragic case of Lizzie Lowe, who took her own life at 14, because she felt she couldn't be both gay and Christian.

These days, I am once more going through the same process of what I want to call de-shaming – this time for a disability I never knew I had. I have recently been diagnosed with ADHD – which stands for attention deficit hyperactivity disorder. It is a type of neurodivergence which affects the pre-frontal cortex of the brain. I have written about the experience of being diagnosed with ADHD on the Inclusive Church blog.[6] The words 'deficit' and 'disorder' are both negative words, which shows that societal prejudice also affects the medical world. In fact, many disabled and neurodivergent people are now arguing for the *social model* of disability. This social model does not pathologize disabled people, as medicine and medical language too often does. It calls on people to talk positively about disability – not talking about disabled people as if we are 'wrong', inadequate or – in some cases – not worthy of life.

Wonderful and helpful as modern medicine is (and I do not want to dismiss the help it gives to all people, including disabled people), it is very much built on a 'problem and cure' mentality, and this can be incredibly damaging to disabled people in society. The social model of disability says that it is above all society which disables people. If there were ramps everywhere and subtitles on films as a matter of course, and if autistic and other neurodivergent people were understood and praised rather than judged and dismissed, perhaps disabled people would feel *enabled* and as if we *fit in* to a society which sees us as gifts rather than problems and burdens. Personally, I am learning to throw off a lifetime of judgement, shame and trauma at being constantly misunderstood, and I am beginning to see that it's society that really has the problem, not me.

Strength in Weakness

It is not only disabled people who have needs. We are all dependent on one another in one way or another at different times in our lives. The fact that society sets disabled people aside in a separate category of 'needy' and burdensome doesn't change that. Individualism and the desire to be totally independent is a false narrative and a dangerous one. Even if we think we don't need anyone now, we will need other people at some point in our lives, especially as we get older.

Part of the reason why disabled people are pitied, looked down on and excluded is because many people don't want to consider their own fragility and dependence on others. The Church is no different in this regard. Despite our faith narrative being built on the vulnerability and weakness of God (no less!), we have always tried to shift the focus of that narrative to be all about the triumphant 'mighty King' and 'all-powerful Lord' etc. Christianity has departed from its radically subversive beginnings which, in the eyes of the world and in the words of St Paul, looked 'foolish', because God triumphed only through weakness, disability[7] and death. Christianity has for too long been perverted into a religion of the strong, the conquerors – the religion of Empire.

The biggest challenge for Christianity now is for it to not

only question but apologize for, *denounce*, and fully reject its imperial past, in order to once more embrace weakness, vulnerability and interdependence as the core of its story and message. It can only achieve this if it listens to and centres the experience of those it has long marginalized and dismissed. Marginalized people are the truth-tellers of Christianity. We are the ones who show the way and who save the Church with our knowledge and insight, just as the woman at the well saved her people, even though they didn't really deserve it for how they'd treated her. Jesus knew she was the key to the salvation of her people. He understood how things really were. She – just like Jesus – was the cornerstone that had been rejected by a society which constantly refuses to 'see' things as they truly are.

Even nowadays, people within the Church refuse to open up to the truth. I have heard many Christians and non-Christians dismiss the kind of work Inclusive Church does as 'identity politics'. This is an expression which is increasingly being used to put marginalized people back in our place, to avoid having to listen to us, to silence us, to make sure we are stopped in our tracks before we can even get started. It can be seen in the way that Black Lives Matter protesters were told they were destroying history when, in reality, they were making it and redeeming it. It can be seen in the way women are told we can't take a joke when we are subjected to sexist attitudes at work. It can be seen in the way that trans women are made out to be perpetrators instead of the victims that they in fact so often are. In truth, it is only people who have enough privilege to not have to question their identity or place in the world who can dismiss marginalized people's struggles for justice as 'identity politics'.

As with so many things, there is another side to all this, though. Labels can be both helpful and unhelpful, depending on the context and how they are used. There are times when a label can put someone in a box and be used against them to say: 'you can't achieve this because you are this'. Similarly, there are times when it is *helpful* to remember that we are all human and have more in common with one another than not. Thirdly, solidarity between marginalized groups is incredibly important, as is the support of allies who are not themselves marginalized. None of us live in identity silos and our identities are complex, not just one single thing.

Having said all that, something must be named in order to be shamed, as the expression goes. We must put something into words and identify it in order to fix the problem that exists. So, saying 'all lives matter' might be true in theory, but it is unhelpful when the point of the expression 'Black lives matter' is to highlight the experience of a group of people whose lives don't currently matter as much as other people's in an inherently racist society. There is a problem which needs to be named – Black lives matter, but society and law enforcement don't act as if they do – in order to be exposed and put right. To respond with 'all lives matter' is similar to dismissing work for justice and inclusion as 'identity politics': it denies that there is a problem and it silences the people who are experiencing injustice and pain.

Conclusion

The Church needs to reject its imperial past, then. It also needs to wake up to the gifts of marginalized peoples, and understand that its calling is to preach a God who suffers exclusion, rejection and death; not a conquering, all-powerful one. Only this can liberate the world and the Church from its obsession with power and strength. The Bible does not tell us that denying our own weakness will set us free or that upholding the status quo will set us free. Only the *truth* can make us free (John 8.32), and the truth is found in relationship, interdependency and the kind of strength which comes from weakness, as Paul identified. It is also found in the love of Christ, which is 'wide and long and high and deep' and which, in the words of liberation theology, has a 'preference for the poor'.

It is both true that God loves everyone the same and that God loves the poor and marginalized preferentially. We can't get our heads round that very easily, but it is true, and the Church needs to reflect and act on it. No theology is more perverse than prosperity gospel theology, which says that God gives wealth and success to those God loves. Wealth and success are not even on God's agenda. Strength in weakness and love for one another are on God's agenda. Centring the most marginalized people is on God's agenda. Moving the centre to the margins is on God's agenda. Saving the Church and the world through those who are ignored and dismissed and considered weak – that is God's agenda. All that the world generally considers foolishness – that is God's agenda.

How can the Church of the future work to undo oppression, including its own long-standing oppression of so many, and centre the experience of marginalized people? There is a charity called Community Peacemaker Teams, which I became involved with in 2011, when I went on a two-week delegation working with and learning from Native American peoples. Prior to that trip, I thought I was very underprivileged – as a woman, and as a gay woman. I had only ever really thought about my own personal experiences and pain, and that is so common for so many of us. I am extremely grateful that I came across CPT at that time in my life, as that two-week trip turned my life upside-down completely and I began to 'see' things I had never seen before.

I was massively privileged. I was white, I was Western, I was brought up in a family that never had to go without money, I was never judged on the colour of my skin or my background or my accent, I had been to university, I had a job. The list went on and on and on. From a place where I was able only to focus on my own pain and marginalization – which was real and should never be dismissed – I was suddenly broken open by listening to the experiences of a group of people who were far more marginalized and hurt than I was. Listening is what changed me – listening to others' experiences. Listening and building a relationship with people. I was suddenly able to empathize more. I was also able to see my own privilege and to wish to dismantle it. This enabled me to become a real agent for change working alongside other marginalized peoples. It awoke in me a solidarity that had until then lain dormant, and the question in my heart became 'What can I do to work alongside you in this struggle?'

My prayer is for the Church to experience that same awakening one day soon. As a Church, we need to not only understand about vulnerability, inclusion, marginalization and justice in an academic way – we need a true conversion of the heart, a repentance, a turning around. We need to recognize Christianity's own part in the violence of Empire, in the narrative of 'might is right' and the over-used narrative of God as the mighty 'Lord over all'. It may be true in one way that God is Lord of all, but in another way the language we use about God can simply end up reinforcing everything that is wrong with the world. The Church needs more humility, more openness to learning, more listening, more awareness, more solidarity, more equality, and more inclusion. That is how it will stay alive in the future, and I will be praying for all our inclusive churches as you participate in building the Kingdom of God. May God be with you all.

Notes

1 This chapter is adapted from a talk given in 2021 to a network of Swedish Lutheran churches. The network is called 'The Future Lives with Us', and it has made a film with English subtitles called *We House the Future*, https://www.youtube.com/watch?v=T81CoOPhsFQ (accessed 15.5.23).

2 https://www.inclusive-church.org/wp-content/uploads/2020/05/22672.pdf (accessed 15.5.23).

3 S. Robertson, 'Sonship in John's Gospel', *Asia Journal of Theology*, 25(2) (Oct. 2011), pp. 315–33.

4 'Mukti's Story' in *Ethnicity: The Inclusive Church Resource Book*, London: Darton, Longman and Todd, 2015.

5 www.scope.org.uk/media/press-releases/brits-feel-uncomfortable-with-disabled-people (accessed 15.5.23).

6 https://www.inclusive-church.org/2020/12/30/on-being-diagnosed-with-adhd-aged-38/ (accessed 15.5.23).

7 See Nancy Eiesland, *The Disabled God: Toward a Liberatory Theology of Disability* (Nashville: Abingdon Press, 1994) for more on Jesus as disabled, both on the cross and after the resurrection.

Epilogue: Beyond Inclusion

NICK BUNDOCK

Please be aware that this chapter has references to suicide and may be upsetting to readers.

Introduction

Lizzie Lowe took her own life in a forgotten patch of farmland behind the River Mersey on 10 September 2014 while her parents were at a film club run by a small group of St James and Emmanuel members. It isn't possible for me to adequately convey the explosion of grief and dismay that hit the Lowes, the church, her school and her wider network of family and friends.

Lizzie Lowe was gay. Nobody in her family or church knew this – how we wish we had! As a 14-year-old girl she was still exploring her feelings and trying to juggle the many powerful emotions of the teenage years, but it was painfully clear from the coroner's hearing in December 2014 that her sexuality and her perception of faith were at odds with each other and had become a chasm too wide to cross. Lizzie had become convinced that God couldn't love her the way she was, a feeling she expressed by text message to the few confidants she had leading up to her fatal decision.

St James and Emmanuel Church has undergone a revolution since Lizzie died. It's not that we were ever 'hard-line'. Actually, we've always been a pretty broad expression of evangelicalism. But, like many similar churches, we've largely avoided the topic of homosexuality in order to preserve the peace. I now realize, too late, that ignoring the topic of sexuality is by definition exclusive and very unsafe for people who are gay. In the time since the coroner's report St James and Emmanuel has been through a revolution. It started with a decision by the PCC to adopt a statement of inclusion. This was followed by three structured 'listening evenings' and inclusion is now a regular item on the agenda of the PCC.

We lost some members during the turmoil of 2015. That was immensely painful as a vicar. But we've also gained members, including a wonderful gay couple who were told not to play in the worship band of their previous church when they found out about their relationship. I can also say that worship in our church has never been more vibrant and alive. Our paradigm shift has swept a new immanence into our worship and a new honesty into our interactions. Personally, I've crossed the Rubicon and there is no way back. When I do look back, I do so with horror at what a spineless and passively homophobic priest I have been.

I don't want anything I've written to sound like a hackneyed 'rags to riches' story, or even a resurrection after death story. There is no way to erase the horror of Lizzie's death, or the sheer madness of the wider Church ripping itself apart over this issue. But I hope our church of St James and Emmanuel in Didsbury has gone some way to amend for our failures. I'm proud to lead a church that is both evangelical and inclusive.

EPILOGUE – BEYOND INCLUSION

Nick Bundock and Ruth Wilde in Conversation

Ruth Wilde: Tell me the story of your church, St James and Emmanuel, Nick.

Nick Bundock: Our story is a good old-fashioned story of repentance. In a good evangelical way! In the opening of Mark's Gospel, it says 'repent and believe' (Mark 1.15). We fell short with the story of Lizzie. It was a safeguarding and sexuality tragedy. We were confronted with the choice. 'The Kingdom of God is at hand' – now what are we going to do? The response when something is at hand is to repent and believe. We could have said, 'Let's just care for the bereaved and make it all about pastoral care. Let's look after those who have been shattered by this death, and let's put the issues that have been raised by this back in the box and avoid confronting them.' That is not repent and believe. That is sweep it under the carpet and limit the damage.

RW: There is a real need for good evangelical theology, isn't there?

NB: Evangelical theology was always meant to be like a single moment as a springboard to hope – a moment of deciding to choose life. That's what grace is. Instead, evangelical theology has become a parody of itself over the years. What Jesus meant by 'repent and believe' is 'I have this amazing thing and all I'm asking you to do is to take hold of it'. He didn't want to say 'I have this terrible burden that you need to take on and you need to whip yourselves for ever. You should all continually excoriate yourselves about your failings and be obsessed with personal morality.' It has become a depressing theology, not a hopeful theology.

We've rediscovered at St James and Emmanuel what it is to be a faithful evangelical church with a positive message of hope and inclusion. The message at Christmas from the angels is 'This is good news for all humanity'. Now I understand what that message means. I look around our church and it is unbelievable these days. The church is so full that there aren't seats for everybody. We talk about how the church is all older women – and there is no problem with that, and we wouldn't have a church without them doing a lot of the work! – but our mix now, because we've opened the church to everyone – it is just so much more balanced. A couple of weeks ago when I was in church, it was heaving. The biggest group of new people is asylum seekers, but I was also giving communion to people with learning difficulties from local sheltered accommodation. Since we've had our new curate – Augustine Tanner-Ihm – who is a gay, Black, American guy – we've found that just having that representation has increased the number of Black families we have in our midst. There are older people, younger people, babies. There is all of humanity. There is a bit in a Psalm where it says that 'all the nations are coming to Zion' and this is what it feels like. I've seen it! I've seen what an inclusive theology can do to transform a church community.

RW: One of the things that growing churches have in common is that they are inclusive, according to recent Methodist research.[1]

NB: They're doing some seriously good work, the Methodists. We have someone doing a PhD on St James and Emmanuel. He's interested in looking at St James and Emmanuel to counter the messages of conservative Christians who say 'go woke go broke' – i.e. a church will die if it becomes inclusive. Andrew is researching our church, because we have seen the exact opposite happening.

The other week I was invited to Chester diocese – very conservative – for their first day on inclusion and diversity. I upset some people, because I thought 'I'm just going to preach it!' At the end of my message, the members of the LGBTQ+ choir that was there came up to me and hugged me. But I also got these spiky emails afterwards from people saying 'you said that and you said this'. Angry emails. The Church has a choice, and it is to 'repent and believe'.

EPILOGUE – BEYOND INCLUSION

RW: Take us through that awful day in 2014.

NB: Lizzie died on 10 September while her mum and dad, Hilary and Kevin, were out at a film night at our church. We had film nights exploring things like the environment or poverty – social justice films. Hilary and Kevin had a social conscience and they liked to be involved with things like that. When they got home, Lizzie wasn't at home. They started calling round to see where she was. Her older brother Michael knew where she often spent time with friends, so they went to this field. It is accessed from behind our church and, although it is a fair way away, the church is the last building before you get to the field. Psychologically, it feels like Lizzie died in the church grounds somehow. Her older brother was the first to find her, and I can't imagine how that must have affected him – the horror. He has a lot of supportive friends, and he is very close to his girlfriend, so they've walked through this together.

Kevin was not far behind Michael. He heard Michael scream, so he knew that something awful had happened. I was in bed at the time probably. This was late at night. They walked back after emergency services arrived on the scene. They stopped off at the house of the associate rector, my colleague Ben Edson, on the way. When I came down in the morning, I saw a message from Ben saying: 'Whatever time of day or night you get this, call me'. A message like that leaves you cold. You know it's not good. When I phoned him, he told me, 'You're going to need to sit down for this.' It's kind of a cliché, but he was right. It was such a shock. I'd had a conversation with Kevin less than two weeks before in the pub, where he'd said, 'How do you cope with the pressures of your job?' and I'd answered, 'It's ok, but the only thing that really cuts me up is the death of a child'. It was very prescient. When I went round to their house, Kevin said 'I can't believe the conversation we were having just a few days ago'. Kevin and Hilary were just in pieces.

I drew up a list of people who I needed to tell, because her parents couldn't bring themselves to do it, and every time I told someone, I just watched them crumble. I had to do that over and again. I likely have PTSD from all of this. I went with them to the mortuary to identify her. I heard them from the next room wailing and I was asked to come in and pray over Lizzie's body. I have never experienced anything so harrowing. It was the hardest period of time I've ever experienced in ministry by a long way.

The police and coroner filed a report in December that year, just before Christmas. The police had taken away laptops and phones to try to find out why this had happened. So Lizzie's parents were experiencing this loss and also the police were also coming in and raiding the house. There was a hearing which I went along to with Hilary and Kevin. There were people from the school there, some of her friends. The verbal report at the hearing said that there was a conflict over her sexuality and faith. There were text messages and friends had given testimonies. There was one Christian group that knew she was gay before she died, and they did what churches and Christians often do – they just ignored it and swept it under the carpet.

The coroner was very gentle with her friends. She sent a text message to one friend saying 'It's going to be World Suicide Prevention Day. How ironic'. Another said, 'God cannot love me this way'. The coroner said to the friends that they couldn't have known. It then came out in the news – it was in the paper because there were reporters present at the hearing. Some conservatives have tried to make out that I made the whole thing up! It was everywhere – in every broadsheet, every newspaper. I was shocked, rocked to my foundations by this, and that was the beginning of the repentance. We weren't even one of these churches where there was a firm line on this. We were eclectic. We wanted everyone to have their own view. There had been some bust-ups over sexuality before my time, so I didn't touch it. After Lizzie's death, though, I realized that we did have to take a stand and not be silent any more.

Silence is deadly, and I can say that from our own bitter experience. If you have come out with a firm line, at least people know where they stand and can make a choice to not attend. We need as churches to have the decency to be upfront about

EPILOGUE – BEYOND INCLUSION

this. Some churches say 'We welcome everyone', but when you dig, you see that they are affiliated to something else which is very hard-line and not inclusive. They are not open about it and people go along and find out further down the line and get hurt.

RW: It's understandable to take the stand of not wanting arguments in the church, but our message to churches out there who might not be taking a stand is please do take a stand, because this is important.

NB: People often ask me to speak to their churches, and something I ask them at the end of the talk is 'If Lizzie was a member of your church, would things have turned out differently?' Most of the time, they look down at their feet and say 'No, it would have been the same, but we've just been lucky that this hasn't happened to us'. We can see what has happened to us, so let the story of Lizzie take the strain for you when you discuss this as a church. The conversations between me and John Bell have been viewed tens of thousands of times.[2] People have emailed me about having a change of heart and becoming inclusive, or more outspoken about inclusion, because of watching the videos. They have sometimes had to leave their churches because they have had a change of heart.

If we hadn't had the media storm and this tragedy on our hands, we might have taken time to discuss what to do as a church. We didn't have this luxury. We took the Inclusive Church statement to the PCC in January – the January after the December hearing. We were in a terrible mess and, although I was criticized for a knee-jerk reaction, we needed to do something and do it urgently. The statement is so beautiful – the IC statement[3] – it is a very evangelical, wonderful statement. It enables the PCC to hold onto threads of continuity and to hold it all together. It's not saying 'out with that and in with this'. It's saying, 'these things that you've always believed, they're still true, but now we're working in a new paradigm of inclusion'. It's genius. It is unequivocal on inclusion, though, and not at all wishy washy. It was passed by the PCC, but it didn't half frighten the horses in the church at large. There was a bit of hoo-ha and some people left. There was even division within the staff team. That was quite painful. I defy anyone in my position to have handled it better though.

Someone who left said, 'You've become nothing more than a glorified social club which stands for nothing. God will take you into exile.' And yet now I see that we *were* in exile and God has taken us back in! We have everyone in our church, and it is thriving. The community at large is there present in the church. We have gathered up the community of God and walked them back out of exile. What I've realized about the terrible state the Church has got itself into is that there are all these people the Church has sent into exile – they would love to be part of the Church, but the Church has excluded them.

Our way into inclusion was through sexuality, but whatever your way into inclusion, once you make it safer for one marginalized group, you make it safer for everyone, every group, even those who you think are not in a marginalized group, because we all have shame and things we struggle with. People feel like they can talk about their struggles now. We've stripped away all of the fake rubbish, all that 'putting your best foot forward' etc. You should be able to put your weak foot forward, to be vulnerable. When you stop having a scapegoat group, everyone is equal, and no one has anything to prove any more. When you have this ideal of perfection, it harms everyone. It is a release to not have to be 'perfect' – for everyone.

RW: You have such a vibrant church with gay, straight, old, young, working class, professional class, refugees, disabled people – everyone is there. Tell me more about the recent developments – for example, Didsbury Pride.

NB: Stage two of the disruption in our church was Didsbury Pride. We had the 'tolerate' stage and then when we decided to do Pride in Didsbury, which was a move into 'celebrate'. It was a shake down, though, because not everyone was happy with this move in the church. What can I say about Didsbury Pride?

EPILOGUE – BEYOND INCLUSION

Oh wow. This year, we had a main stage, bands playing all afternoon, thousands of people in the church grounds. It's this amazing atmosphere and there are clergy everywhere with their dog collars on. I got up on the main stage this year and there was cheering. I said 'I'm not going to preach a sermon. There is a verse in the Bible which I love, and it says, "God is love and those who live in love live in God." That's what I'd say to you today.' They just erupted! You know what, in Acts it said there were 3,000 people listening to Peter on the day of Pentecost. I thought, 'there are 3,000 people here listening to me talking about the love of God'. That is what evangelism looks like now. It's natural and exciting and it's not weird and jarring and awkward. That was it; that was the message. There was not a single person in that place who went away knowing less about God. They all went away knowing more about the love of God than when they turned up.

RW: You're right about the awkwardness. For example, the Church is so weird in the way it tries to go about forcing people into church to get their kids into church schools. I've realized how odd this is since we've been looking round schools for my son who's just turned four. The Church needs to trust in its gift and to trust the Holy Spirit. Open the doors of church schools to all and trust in the gift, the precious gift that is faith. So many people still need it and still want to have a faith. Some of those children will find that gift at school and will carry it forward in their lives because it will become meaningful and helpful to them. Faith is still so important today, but the Church is trying to force people into having a faith, getting atheists to go to church for their child to go to school. It's just awkward and jarring – like you said. Let's just stop being weird!

NB: That is absolutely right. The braver we are and the more open-hearted we are, the most authentic and powerful the message. I've found that also with scripture. Just dare to believe that grace keeps going on and on and on. My understanding of scripture has changed. People will say that I've thrown it out.

It's not true. In fact, it's come alive for me in so many ways. My eyes have been opened to this great story. The whole of scripture is a story of emancipation. There's the bit in Acts where God says, 'Don't call unclean what I call clean'.[4] Accepting the Gentiles into the Church then was radical. You could easily have argued from scripture to exclude Gentiles – despite there being passages of acceptance, there were also passages which excluded Gentiles. It was radical to accept and include. God is still saying this to us – that was just the start. God says to us: 'Keep including'.

There's the passage where Paul says, 'There is no Jew nor Gentile, slave nor free, nor is there male or female, for you are all one in Christ Jesus'.[5] I was speaking recently on this passage and I continued it on 'and there is no gay or straight, non-binary, trans etc.' Keep going! Paul couldn't possibly have understood everything about human sexuality, but it's the trajectory. Scripture hasn't been thrown away for me; it's been enlivened!

RW: It is in the Jewish tradition to have the argument present even within scripture. Jesus himself argues with scripture. There are some writers in scripture who are more conservative, saying 'don't intermarry with non-Jews', but then there are books like Ruth which show someone important to God's story – a great-grandmother of Jesus – being a Gentile and marrying into a Jewish family. I like how the Jewish faith just keeps that argument in there in the scriptures. I feel like it's an invitation to us to argue and wrestle with scripture too, as Jesus did. Nick, what's your nightmare scenario and what's your hope scenario for the Church?

NB: I can only authentically speak for the Church of England. My nightmare for the Church of England is that it doesn't live up to its name. The vision of the Church of England is to be a Church for everyone – as it says in the name. My nightmare is that it becomes a narrow sect of true believers. There is a struggle and it is pulling in both directions. I believe in the concept of the Church being for everyone, and that's the prize for the Church of England. That's what it can be. At the moment, I have faith and believe that is where we'll end up, but my nightmare is the opposite – that we'll end up like a sect. The hopeful scenario is a Church for everyone. It is so energizing. To call people who are very different to you family is such a lovely thing, and it enhances difference. When people are different to you it's not a threat, it's a beautiful thing. I'm different too – to them. We see difference and similarity in each other's faces. That's when we see the image of God. When I see my gay friends, my trans friends, my Black friends, my refugee friends, my friends with learning disabilities, their faces and our faces complete the image of God. What an incredible vision that is. It's an eschatological vision of what humanity is and it is the image of God.

Notes

1 https://www.inclusive-church.org/wp-content/uploads/2020/05/22672.pdf (accessed 15.5.23).
2 https://stjamesandemmanuel.org/beyond-inclusion/ (accessed 15.5.23).
3 See the home page of the IC website: www.inclusive-church.org (accessed 15.5.23).
4 Acts 11.9.
5 Galatians 3.28.

Index

access, to power 13–16
Achebe, Chinua 48
angels 3–4
Austen, Jane 48–9, 50

Bartimaeus 6–8
Beckford, Robert 49
body of Christ 91
Brueggemann, Walter 20

Callaghan, Bob xiv, 1, 59–60
Christian Aid, support for women 43–5
church growth 5
climate change 41–2
Community Peacemaker Teams 105
Cone, James 49–50
Covid lockdown, and worship 88–9

Dawkins, Richard 93
Didsbury Pride 114–15
disability 58–71
 attitudes to 4, 6–9
disruption, in worship 85–7, 93–4

Eadie, Donald 64–5
eucharist 17–19
exclusion, from the Church 2–3
expansive love 16–18

faces 88
family planning 39
fear, of difference 4–6, 62
Floyd, George 47–8
Fraser, Giles xiii, xiv

gender, pronouns 73–5
gender equality 32–45
gender neutral spaces 76
generosity 16–18
Gerrish, Brian 15–16
Gilroy, Paul 51
God, gender neutral language for 76
Goddard, Giles xiv
Gwilliams, Dianna xiv

healing 7–9
Herbert, Clare xiv, 59–60
Hodson, Mims 62
Holy Communion 17–18
hospitality 85

Hull, John 60, 63, 64–5
The Hundred-Foot Journey
  (film) 12–13

identity politics 19
image of God 76, 93, 117
inclusion
  church statements on 108,
    113–16
  what it is 1–9
Inclusive Church
  disability conferences 58–71
  origins xiii–xv

Jennings, Willie James 47, 50
Jesus
  at table 16
  command to love
    neighbours 78–9
  and disabled people 6–9
  and gender justice 37–8
  imagined as white 51–2, 55
John, Jeffrey xiii

Keller, Catherine 21
Kenya, tax system 41
Kim, Yung-Suk 20
Kingdom of God 93, 97
Kingdom of Heaven 84
Kings College Cambridge 91

Laudato Si' 21
LGBTQ+ people
  diversity among 27
  groups hosted by churches
    75–6
  reactions to 4

listening 98, 105–6, 108
love of God 115
Lowe, Lizzie 107–12

MacMillan, Fiona xiv
marginalized groups 13–14
Mary Magdalene 87–8
meals 11–13
minority groups 13–14
mission Christianity 52–5
music 87, 91–2
mystery 20–1

neurodiversity 67–8
Noël, Rachel 67–8, 86
non-binary people 74

'one in Christ' 18–19
otherness 3–6

perfection 84–5, 91, 94, 114
Pointed Land allegory 81–3
poverty, and gender 32
power 13–15
pride flags 78
privilege 13–15
pronouns (personal) 73–5

queer theory 90–2, 96 n.5

race 56
Richardson, Emily 65–6
Roman Catholic Church,
  attitudes to sexual
  diversity 23–31
Roy, Arundhati 15

INDEX

St James and Emmanuel (Didsbury) 107–15
St Martin-in-the-Fields 61, 69
Schirr, Bertram 91–2
sexuality, ignored 108, 112
silence 19–21
singing 87, 91–2
Sistine Chapel 93
Smith, Gwendolyn Ann 77
Stonewall 23–31
Sugirtharajah, R. S. 56
Swinton, John 62

table space 13–21
taxation 40–1
tradition 11, 15–16
trans people 28–30, 72–9
Transgender Day of Remembrance 77
transphobia 79

United Reformed Church 11–12

VAT 40–1
vulnerability 38, 68, 92, 94

Wells, Ruth, poems by 89–90
Wells, Sam 61
whiteness 47–57
Williams, Rowan 17, 20
Wilson, Rachel 60
women
  discrimination against 39–42
  in the Gospels 37
  and poverty 32–4, 41
  sexual violence 38–9
words, insufficiency of 19–21
worship
  disruption 85–7, 93–4
  during Covid lockdown 88–9

Young, Jane 60